MARELLA AGNELLI | THE LAST SWAN

MARELLA AGNELLI
THE LAST SWAN

MARELLA AGNELLI

&

MARELLA CARACCIOLO CHIA

RIZZOLI
NEW YORK

New York · Paris · London · Milan

CONTENTS

INTRODUCTION

THERE SOMETIMES COMES A MOMENT IN LIFE, ESPECIALLY IF IT IS ONE AS LONG AND EVENTFUL as Marella Agnelli's, in which one feels the need to look back and try to make sense of it all. This is the substance of what John Elkann, Gianni and Marella Agnelli's eldest grandson, said to me in 2011. That conversation was the genesis of this book. During the following three years, slowly at first but gathering pace as we went along, my aunt Marella and I have spent many hours together looking at thousands of photographs. Some came out of the Agnelli private archive in Turin. Others were found by scouring the archives of twentieth-century photographers whose portraits of Marella, from the 1940s onward, transformed her into a modern symbol of timeless beauty and elegance. Another source of images was the Condé Nast archives in New York.

Gathering these long-lost photographs was a powerful catalyst in bringing memories to the surface. If some are tinged with sadness, others are filled with laughter and good humor. All of them have led Marella, a riveting storyteller, to share anecdotes about the people and places that have made a lasting impression on her. These stories, together with others found in past interviews, are woven into the narrative of this book.

The focus here is on the Agnelli houses and gardens. In the sixty or so years since her marriage to

Gianni Agnelli, in 1953, Marella has worked side by side with outstanding architects, designers, and gardeners, many of whom have been interviewed for this book, and created homes in the mountains, by the sea, in rural areas, and in cities north and south of the Mediterranean and on both sides of the Atlantic. Some of them, such as the Milan apartment portrayed in Ugo Mulas's 1969 shoot, were photographed soon after completion and all of them have been shot by some of the greatest garden and interiors photographers of our time. Which is why this book is much more than a personal memoir. It is a small anthology recording how our way of looking at—and photographing—gardens and interiors have evolved during the course of sixty years. Many of the photos in this book are being published for the first time.

I will conclude with a personal anecdote about Marella. It dates back to 1993 when she and I, together with a friend of ours, Annina Migone, traveled to the Bordeaux region for a week-long retreat led by Thich Nhat Hanh, the author of *The Miracle of Mindfulness*. One of the requirements was that each person would contribute to the community work. Some cleaned, some cooked, some took care of the children. Marella decided she would be in charge of breakfast. Each morning she would wake up at the crack of dawn to set up dozens of places, adding little touches like handpicked flowers in glasses of water. Afterward, she cleared everything in a flash and scrubbed the tables clean. This dedication, as testified by those who worked with her on one or other of her projects, is a constant trait of hers. Anything she undertakes—whether it be planting or photographing a garden, designing a line of fabric, or creating an interior—she will carry forward with focused passion. "*Il faut cultiver son jardin*," she often said to me in French, quoting Voltaire, as I was growing up. The implication is that the foundation of all things beautiful, even the most impermanent, is dedication and hard work. This book, as John Elkann anticipated, is tangible proof of that. There is not a picture or a sentence in here that Marella hasn't toiled over. But it was worth it. The making of it has been a labor of love, and of happiness, for both of us.

—MARELLA CARACCIOLO CHIA

DONNA MARELLA
CARACCIOLO DI CASTAGNETO

A young Marella Caracciolo in the garden of Villa I Cancelli, her
parents' house in Florence, circa 1946.

I WAS BORN IN THE FOUR-POSTER BED IN MY PARENTS' BEDROOM AT I CANCELLI, A sixteenth-century villa on the hills overlooking Florence. It was on the fourth of May 1927. My brother Carlo had been born in that same room some eighteen months earlier and Nicola, our younger brother, made his first appearance there four years later. I still remember many details of my parents' bedroom on the first floor of the villa: the crackling fireplace, the south-facing windows overlooking the garden and the hills, the pink gauze curtains flowing in the breeze. . . . My mother spent a great deal of her time in this room reading books on philosophy and theology, a soft cover of pink marabou feathers draping her legs.

My mother, Margaret Clarke, was beautiful, intelligent, and complicated. There were no pre-ordained timetables at home and there was often a sense of experimental precariousness. My mother had a developed aesthetic sense but no interest at all in domesticity. Whenever we traveled, however, she would open a trunk and bring out piece after piece of magnificent fabric to drape over sofas and lamps. She would fill the vases with flowers. Thanks to her, those anonymous rooms became immediately beautiful and familiar to us.

My mother was an American from Peoria, Illinois. Her father, Charles, belonged to a family of old Puritan stock that had made a considerable fortune with Clarke Bros. & Co., a whiskey distillery that claimed to be the largest in the world, though this was an exaggeration. His father had been a close friend of President Lincoln, and Charles, who was elected mayor of Peoria twice, was known for his enlightened policies and public administration. He died young, when my mother was a child.

In the aftermath of World War I, my mother, who was then twenty-one, moved to Europe with her much-older half sister, Mary, and their mother, Alice Chandler Clarke—London first, *then Paris, and finally Florence, where she eventually met her husband to be, Filippo Caracciolo di Melito, my father. He was a handsome officer seven years younger than she, with a passion for writing and poetry.*

The first garden I remember is the one belonging to I Cancelli, the villa my brothers and I grew up in. My grandmother, following in the steps of other Anglo-American expatriates, had bought this villa surrounded by olive groves for my mother in 1923. The garden was divided into many "rooms," which we children named. The thick vegetation near the pond, fascinating and mysterious, became "the jungle" while the fruit orchard was the "pomario." Then there was "Grandma Clarke's garden." I had not met my American grandmother, who died two years before I was born, but her garden, which was surrounded by tall walls of clipped laurel and filled with colorful herbaceous borders, was my favorite. It had a bright blue wooden bench at its center, like in a painting by the Viennese Secessionist Carl Moll. It was the most romantic part of the garden, which is why I liked it so much. Hoping

to please me, my parents had renamed another area "Marella's garden." It was classical in style, all clipped boxwood and white gravel. I found "Marella's garden" desperately ugly and longed for Grandma Clarke's one instead.

Another childhood home I loved was one my mother had built in the mountains near Brixen, in the Italian Dolomites. It was a plain two-story house with spectacular mountain views and a stream running past it. With the help of Gino, our gardener from Florence, my mother created terraced gardens that she filled with dog roses and wildflowers. All around it was a forest of pine trees, chestnuts, and beeches. As children, we would spend every summer there going for long walks, riding bicycles, swimming in the local pool. There was a large terrace furnished with wicker chairs and tables.

My mother had taste. Her houses were elegant and cozy. A vague sense of disorder pervaded every room but there was also a great attention to detail: vases filled with freshly picked flowers, embroidered bed linens, an attention to each day's menus, things like that.

As a child, I remember having roaring fights with her over the decoration of my bedroom. I liked some paintings, while she preferred others. She loved pale blue; I wanted nothing but pink. I was very stubborn and in the end my mother succumbed.

My father, Filippo, was not so interested in these aesthetic disquisitions. What he longed to do was write and when he was young he published several novels and a few collections of poetry. The financial crash of 1929, however, badly affected my mother's fortune and so my father applied for a post in the diplomatic service. I think he was the first member of his family to have a proper job: traditionally members of the old southern aristocracy, like him, rarely worked for a living. So off we went to Ankara, Turkey, where we lived for most of the late 1930s.

In Turkey I was allowed to adopt all of the district's stray dogs. I took care of them, fed them, gave each one of them a name. When we left, in 1939, I had to leave them behind—all of them except one, Tommaso. I was deeply grieved. As an adult I have continued to seek the company of dogs, always. This passion of mine was something I shared with Gianni. We had all kinds of dogs: Labradors, Huskies, mongrels. Dogs offer great companionship and I am convinced that their loyalty and purity protect us. I had a German shepherd once who looked over my children for many years. His name was Makyu and he was a gift from my brother-in-law Umberto.

When the war broke out, my father was appointed Italian general consul in Lugano, Switzerland. It was during that time that he made contact with the Partito d'Azione, an anti-Fascist political movement supported by the Allies. My father, who spoke perfect English, was a liaison agent who kept in constant touch with the British secret service.

DURING THE SUMMER OF 1943 I REMEMBER climbing out of the windows at night to look at the glare in the sky from the bombings of Milan. It was a terrifying spectacle.

Our home, conveniently close to the Italian border, became a meeting point for members of the Italian resistance movement, who met there

Caracciolo family photographs include portraits of Marella; her parents, Filippo and Margaret Caracciolo di Melito; and her older and younger brothers, Carlo and Nicola; as well as a view of the family villa near Brixen, in northern Italy. Leonor Fini painted the portrait of Margaret Caracciolo, Princess of Castagneto.

with members of the American Office of Strategic Services (OSS). After the armistice, my father left for Naples and, at the end of an adventurous journey, he joined other members of the Partito d'Azione. In the summer of 1944 my brother Carlo, who was eighteen years old, joined the underground resistance movement. He tried to get used to life in the wilderness by camping out in our back garden. He was gone for many months, until he was arrested by the Fascists and narrowly escaped execution.

It was in Switzerland during the war that I first met Virginia Agnelli, Gianni's mother. It must have been 1943, and she had come over the border to the village of Villar-sur-Ollon to visit some of her children, who were staying with friends. In the 1930s the Agnellis, and especially Virginia and her husband Edoardo, who died in a plane accident in 1935, had been at the center of what was known then as the "fast set." They led a glamorous life of parties, streamlined yachts, fast cars, and luxurious villas. Like most members of that set, they kept lovers. Their lives filled the gossip columns. I wouldn't say they belonged to an

immoral world, just a freely amoral one. At least by comparison to the one I had grown up in, an isolated, slightly conservative world known as the anglo-beceri *and inhabited mainly by wealthy Anglo-American expatriates, like my mother, and members of the old Italian aristocracy, like my father—a set of people who spent their days visiting one another's exquisitely refined gardens and crumbling villas on the hills of Florence and getting into interminable philosophical disquisitions.*

The Agnellis represented a new and exciting lifestyle. So that day, when I was introduced to Virginia for the first time, I looked at her with fascination and found her elegant and beautiful. She was only forty-three years old but I perceived her as an old woman. She wore her graying hair cropped short, which I found very chic. She died in a car crash two years later.

It was after that first brief encounter that I began to listen to stories about the Agnelli clan and about Gianni, the eldest son. My girlfriends spent hours telling me about his reckless military actions as well as his gallant bravery. These narratives of heroic and irreverent behavior filled my imagi-

nation during those last war-torn years with a kind of longing. It was at that time, I think, that without ever even having met Gianni, I started to feel butterflies fluttering for him.

Maria Sole, one of Gianni's younger sisters, and I were friends. We had several things in common including the fact that we were both convinced that we owned the most beautiful feet in the world. One day Maria Sole brought me a present: a pair of evening shoes that had belonged to Virginia. I was over the moon with happiness. They had been handmade by Cavalera, the famous shoemaker in Turin. I still remember them distinctly: they were red satin with a tiny bow embroidered to one side and black heels. Imagine what they meant to me. I was seventeen years old and had spent all the war years, from the time I was thirteen, wearing big mountain boots or shoes with cork heels. I think that's why, in later years, I turned into a shoe fetishist. I have never forgotten those red satin shoes.

AFTER THE WAR, WE RETURNED TO FLORence for a brief period. *I still cringe when I am made to remember the time I was elected Miss Florence, in 1947. It all started with a night out with my brother Carlo and some friends. We ended up in a club where Miss Florence was being elected. I was sitting at one of the tables with my friends when suddenly someone in the jury indicated me: I found myself unexpectedly pulled onto the stage, the scepter of Miss Florence thrust into my hand!*

Making my way back home later that evening, I felt mortified. I took the bus with Carlo and our friends but got off halfway because I was just too frightened to return home. I was afraid my parents would be very disappointed in me. In those years, you see, une fille de bonne famille—*a respectable girl—could not even dream of becoming a "Miss." My parents tried to stop the news from coming out in the press the next day but they did not succeed. They never uttered a word about it after that—I still don't know whether it was out of discretion or embarrassment. In any case, one year later my family and I moved to Rome.*

Growing up is always difficult. One has identity crises, one is this, one is that, one is always

Opposite: Marella with friend and future sister-in-law Maria Sole Agnelli (bottom left), Franca Spalletti (upper left), and Rosine Carcano (upper right).

Above: Marella with Count Alvise di Robilant (on left) and Nicky Pignatelli. All photographs (except opposite, bottom right) were taken in the summer of 1953 at Villa Reale di Marlia, Lucca, by CAMILLA PECCI BLUNT MCGRATH.

Marella at Positano, 1948. Photograph by PRINCE ENRICO D'ASSIA.

in love. There is a terrible confusion. What made me happy then? Not love—I was too impatient, and love was a terrible torment. I often spent entire afternoons reading poetry: Rimbaud, Verlaine, Baudelaire. School? Far too boring. I did love to draw. Everything visual filled me with real pleasure, even more than reading. Looking at nature, quietly contemplating something beautiful filled me with joy. Which is why in 1949 I went off to Paris to study drawing and theater design at the Académie Julian.

IN ITALY AT THAT TIME THERE WERE VERY very few things a young, unmarried girl could do. Marriage, of course, was the main option but that was not in the cards then, and so what to do? There was only one way out: le grand depart, le grand oubli. My parents supported this.

Unlike many of my girlfriends, I had a liberal education. My Italian grandmother, Meralda, longed to see me married off as soon as possible to some grand and wealthy aristocrat, but my parents did not seem to care about that.

They were modern in this way—it may have been the influence of my mother's American background. After my Parisian interlude as an art student, I told them I wanted to go to New York. It was 1950 and I was twenty-three. They said fine, as long as I find a job and earn some money, which I did.

In the early 1950s, the American Dream had captured the minds of my generation and nowhere did this dream feel more alive—in art, in fashion, in film, in literature—than in New York City. So when the great photographer Erwin Blumenfeld offered me a job as a model, although I found it extremely boring to pose for photographs, I grabbed it.

One day, seeing that I seemed far more interested in the technical aspects of photography such as lighting than makeup or clothes, Blumenfeld said to me, "Maybe it's time for you to pass onto this side of the camera?" That's when I became his assistant. This meant keeping his studio tidy and his camera, a Rolleiflex, in good working order. In between these chores he taught me to take pictures.

There were many excellent photographers in New York in those years: Dick Avedon, the genius of portraits; Irving Penn, whose unique way of working with color and light gave him the aura of a magician. But no one, I think, had Blumenfeld's courage and desire to experiment. Every picture, for him, was a new territory that would come to life in the darkness of his camera obscura. We spent hours in the darkroom perfecting some of his iconic compositions, such as the surreal image of three mouths.

HOW DID GIANNI AND I MEET? IT FEELS AS *if I have always known him, but the truth is that we met shortly after the war through his sisters. I must have been eighteen or so and Gianni was six years older. Our love affair was on and off for several years before we got engaged to marry.*

The Agnellis—seven siblings who all looked alike, talked alike, and often laughed at the same jokes—emanated a tribal aura. And they had a myriad of cousins. Edoardo and Virginia Agnelli had died young, so Gianni, at twenty-four, found himself the head of the family. His

Pages 20–21: Marella Caracciolo di Castagneto, wearing a gown by Gabriella Sport and holding a watercolor by Leonor Fini, circa 1952–53; portrait of Marella, 1952–53. Photographs by ARTURO GHERGO in his Rome studio.

Opposite: Mrs. Edward Behn and Marella Caracciolo di Castagneto (right), both in gowns by Gabriella Sport, in a Roman ballroom, 1949. Photograph by CLIFFORD COFFIN.

Portrait of Marella, 1951. Photograph by
ERWIN BLUMENFELD in his New York studio.

youngest brother, Umberto, was only eleven at the time. Gianni was very close to all his siblings and so when he and I got engaged, in the late summer of 1953, I felt daunted at the prospect of having to take on such a large, clannish family. But everyone was very supportive of us, including the devoted house staff that had served the Agnelli family for decades. They were delighted that, at the age of thirty-two, their Avvocato, as they called him in tribute to his law degree, had finally decided to get married.

When Gianni came to Rome to see my parents and ask for my hand, as one did in those days, I was in a state of total anxiety. I think I may have even stood behind the closed doors trying to eavesdrop. My mother wasn't enthusiastic about this marriage at first. Her Puritan streak made her wary of the Agnelli glamour and she didn't like the fact that Gianni was a fixture in the gossip columns. My father was less judgmental and gave our union a chance.

Opposite and pages 28–30: Donna Marella Caracciolo di Castagneto, wearing a white satin dress by Balenciaga, marries Gianni Agnelli in the chapel of Osthoffen Castle, just outside Strasbourg, on November 19, 1953. Photographs by ROBERT DOISNEAU.

WE WERE MARRIED ON NOVEMBER 19, 1953, in the chapel of Osthoffen Castle, just outside of Strasbourg. My father, at the time, was secretary-general of the Council of Europe, which was based in that city. The day of our wedding was cold and gray but the house was full of life. Our two families were there—including my Caracciolo cousins, uncle, and aunt—as well as our closest friends, some sixty people in all. I wore a Balenciaga gown. Gianni was on crutches following a bad car accident the year before. My mother organized everything to perfection. She tended to be disorganized in the management of her everyday life, and on the whole she avoided social events, but when she had to, she was amazing.

Vogue *sent Robert Doisneau to shoot our wedding day. He was so discreet that I actually don't even remember him being there. He took some marvelous pictures, though.*

VILLA AGNELLI, VILLAR PEROSA

FILIPPO JUVARRA | STÉPHANE BOUDIN | RUSSELL PAGE

When the twenty-six-year-old Marella Caracciolo first set foot in Villar Perosa as Gianni's fiancée, in September of 1953, what impressed her most was not the villa's graceful Baroque architecture but—as she would recall years later—the well-honed atmosphere of a real family home.

"Villar Perosa has always been central to my life, ever since I was a child," Gianni Agnelli said during a conversation that took place in April 1997 at his home in Turin. "Every year in August twelve children—my six siblings and I, plus our five cousins—would invade our grandparents' summer retreat and stay there until the middle of September. Our days in Villar were molded by sports and a rigid sense of discipline imparted to us by a string of English governesses. Punctuality was of paramount importance. Villar was more than a summer retreat. It was a way of life. An education."

Attributed to Filippo Juvarra, one of the masters of Piedmontese Baroque architecture, Villar Perosa was built in the early eighteenth century as a hunting lodge for Vittorio Amedeo II, the first king of the Savoy dynasty. Giuseppe Agnelli, an ex-army man who had made his fortune cultivating silkworms, bought it in 1811.

Perched high on a hill overlooking the Val Chisone, halfway between the Po Valley and the

Rear view of Villa Agnelli as seen from the cutting garden, resplendent with red dahlias, 1967. Photograph by HORST P. HORST.

Alps, the villa's symmetrical façade stands out against a backdrop of thickly planted forests. From its arched entrance, one accesses the grand double staircase leading up to the gallery on the first floor, an exuberant network of painted stucco vaulted ceilings, chinoiserie-style painted wallpaper, and ornate garlands heralding the approach of the rococo style.

In the early 1950s M. Stéphane Boudin, the Parisian interior decorator of Maison Jansen fame who put his signature on all the great houses of Europe from 1930 onward, including those belonging to the Duke and Duchess of Windsor, was asked to restore a wing of Villar Perosa that had been damaged during World War II. Though the villa's interiors were refurnished in the colorful eighteenth-century Piedmontese style, in some rooms Marella imposed her trademark straw matting and wicker furniture upholstered in bright patterns.

As for the garden, Russell Page, the British gardener, was summoned. "Wherever there was level ground," he wrote disapprovingly in his 1962 memoir, *The Education of a Gardener*, "there was a formal box parterre, six of them, some terraced and all set out with endless rows of ugly terracotta vases and white marble fountains and statues. For years the gardener had been planting conifers and adding odd beds, usually full of scarlet salvias and geraniums. When I arrived he had been there for over fifty years." It took Marella and Russell several years to reveal the garden's underlying eighteenth-century structure and open up the vistas. They tore through the thick vegetation in the hollow of the estate's narrow valley and transformed its stream into a series of lakes.

After the British gardener's death in 1985, landscape architect and author Paolo Pejrone continued to work there much in the same spirit. The two had met at the Agnellis' home in Turin during a snowstorm in January of 1970 and Pejrone, a young architect at the time, eventually became the only disciple Page ever had. "Villar has continued to evolve and expand during the decades," Pejrone said during an interview in October 2013. "In time, Marella developed her own vision marked by a bold sense of color. We had a lot of fun working together and if Russell could see the garden now, I think he would be surprised. Pleasantly surprised."

Gianni Agnelli, behind the wheel of a car, surrounded by his siblings and a family dog, at Villar Perosa, early 1930s.

I HAVE A VIVID MEMORY OF WHEN I *visited Villar Perosa for the first time. It was during the days leading up to Maria Sole's wedding to Ranieri di Campello. Each morning, as soon as I woke up, a splendid breakfast on a tray was brought to my bedroom. All the silver—the coffeepot, the milk jug, the cutlery—had been polished to perfection. It felt as if I had stepped into an enchanted place where time had been suspended. Everything was so tranquil, so serene. The older generations had passed away but their presence was still felt. I can still see the cleaning ladies wearing their old-fashioned uniforms with long aprons and embroidered camisoles, their hair held up in tight chignons.*

Left: Marella, in silk *Pyjama Palazzo* by Valentino, in the *salone dipinto*, the painted room, 1967. Photograph by HORST P. HORST.

Pages 38–39: View of the villa's front façade. Photograph by FRANÇOIS HALARD.

THERE WERE OTHER HOUSES PERHAPS

grander and more beautiful, like La Leopolda,

but Villar had this connection to the past that was

very tender. I liked everything about it, even the

lapses of taste, such as the overwhelming presence

of palm trees, so unnatural for a garden near the

Alps, or the borders made of chunky white char-

coal filled with sage and bright, colorful plants.

Opposite: Detail of the double staircase, designed circa 1730 by architect Filippo Juvarra.

Pages 42–43: The Chinese gallery on the *piano nobile*. Photographs by OBERTO GILI.

IN 1954, WHEN I FIRST MET HIM, *M. Stéphane Boudin was an affable man at the peak of his career as an interior decorator. Maison Jansen, the internationally acclaimed decoration firm based in Paris, revolved around him completely. More to the point, M. Boudin was Maison Jansen!*

Together we set out to restore the eighteenth-century "chinoiserie" gallery, to refresh the upholstery and paintwork, and to open up the arched loggia on the first floor. We also fitted the villa with all the amenities one would expect in the mid-twentieth century but without tarnishing its lovely, ancient patina.

Pages 44–45: Marella's private reading room.

Opposite: The garden room on the ground floor, with wicker furniture by Vittorio Bonacina. Photographs by OBERTO GILI.

ONE DAY I ASKED M. BOUDIN IF HE HAD someone in mind for the garden. "Russell Page," was his answer. I was thrilled when I heard this name because I had admired his work in a garden near Paris. The first thing that struck me about Russell, when he first came to meet us at Villar, was his magnificent enormity. He was a giant. Within a few moments of meeting him, I also realized he was a man of great talent. His main preoccupation was not that of making a beautiful garden but of harmony. The idea that a garden had to be connected to the surrounding landscape was a modern concept back then, and one I embraced wholeheartedly.

That first evening, before dinner was served, M. Boudin, Gianni, Russell, and I were sitting in the open portico on the first floor, where drinks were being served. Russell and I moved over toward the railing to look at the garden at sunset. It was a glorious June evening, I remember, and we could hear the croaking of the frogs in the nearby ponds. It was at that moment that Page uttered words that surprised me and struck a deep chord within. "One must learn," he said, referring to the dangers of living with a great fortune, "to serve something higher than us all, because if not, one may easily fall slave to the basest, most material aspects of one's life." I felt an instant rush of sympathy toward him. He was a deeply spirited individual with an interest in Sufism and other Eastern philosophies. He had married the daughter of Gurdjeff, a well-known guru at the beginning of the twentieth century.

Those first few days in Villar we spent exploring every corner of the garden. Russell took notes and made sketches—this was his way of memorizing. He touched the earth and the plants; he liked to get his hands dirty. His priority, he said, was to get rid of all the nineteenth-century redundancies. The cherubic fountains, red sage borders, and palm trees horrified him. He was a purist.

View of the villa's gardens with manicured lawns, clipped boxwood, and raked gravel paths, 1967. Photograph by HORST P. HORST.

49

RUSSELL DID HAVE A SIXTH SENSE ABOUT *gardens. Once we considered ways of redesigning the back lawn. We had agreed to eliminate a fountain and some mediocre statues and to plant boxwood hedges in clear-cut geometrical patterns. But all this wasn't enough for him. He kept pointing out the back wall exclaiming, "This is not right! It just doesn't look right!" He was so insistent that, in the end, he convinced me. Soon after the first stones were removed, we discovered the remains of a much older wall placed at a much more balanced angle to the house and the gardens.*

Recovering a sense of balance and harmony was at the core of Russell's philosophy as a gardener, and I adhered to this pursuit of classical elegance. His choices were informed by a deep knowledge of the history of gardening as well as the provenance of plants. At Villar we simplified the structure and made it stronger and more clear-cut. Most importantly, we extended and blurred the confines of the garden so that the surrounding wilderness became an integral part of it.

Opposite: View of the cutting garden and greenhouse as seen from the villa's top floor.

Pages 52–53: Rose garden contained by a boxwood hedge.

Pages 54–55: Russell Page designed the bridge in 1956 in the manner of the Anglo-Chinese style of William Chambers. The century-old trees are mostly beech. Photographs by FRANÇOIS HALARD.

WHAT I REGARD AS OUR GREATEST achievement in Villar Perosa is the valley we call i laghi, "the lakes." Running down its center was a torrent of water. Thick woods and bramble bushes made the area inaccessible so we cleared it up and built several dams to channel the stream's water into small lakes and ponds, each one a little different in size and shape. We planted this area with a rich combination of local and exotic water plants.

Russell's use of water was one of his strengths as a gardener. He described his feelings of bliss when, while traveling in the Middle East, he sat quietly by the water in the court of an old mosque and felt himself replenished by the accumulated peace wrought by centuries of prayers. Water, he explained, symbolized the idea of a conscious, elevated spirit in nature.

When we first started work on Villar Perosa, Russell was excited at the prospect of creating an alpine garden using local plants. As time went by, however, we were replacing exotic plants with even more exotic ones.

Years later, Russell came to pay us a visit. During a walk I asked him, "But Russell, whatever happened to your idea of creating a spontaneous garden of native plants?" "Ah . . ." he answered with an enigmatic smile, "but Villar is different from other gardens . . . it is my Shangri-la."

Pages 56–57: The nineteenth-century water cistern, designed to mimic a medieval tower, is on the lawn in front of the villa and has served as a playhouse for generations of Agnelli children. The Russell Page–designed path leads away from the main entrance and toward the end of the garden. The tree to the right is a monkey tree and the one to the left a thuja.

Opposite: A view of the villa's facade as seen from the expansive arboretum.

Pages 60–61: A view of the lake area, designed by Russell Page in the mid-1950s. The stream was turned into a series of lakes and filled with water lilies, water irises, and ferns. Photographs by FRANÇOIS HALARD.

I WAS SO DELIGHTED TO BE GIVEN THE *opportunity to learn from Russell that I did not dare, at first, to oppose his vision. But the truth is I couldn't bear to see all those old trees being torn down. When I started to put my foot down in their defense, the fights began. One I remember vividly occurred over a small forest of fir trees that used to enclose the garden at the rear of the villa. Aniceta Agnelli, Gianni's great-grandmother, had planted it to introduce some wilderness into the garden. By the time Russell saw it, it had grown into a massive green wall that blotted out the views. Without consulting me, he gave orders to have it chopped down. I was livid when I found out! I could not accept the way he would knock out things and trees that had been there for generations. Russell, on the other hand, saw the garden from a purely aesthetic point of view and scoffed at what he considered my sentimentality.*

Opposite: An eighteenth-century statue of the goddess Diana with flowering cherry blossoms.

Pages 64–65: Terraced eighteenth-century gardens flanked by Japanese flowering cherry trees. Photographs by MARELLA AGNELLI.

DURING THE 1950S, WHEN OUR CHILDREN, *Edoardo and Margherita, were young, we used to spend several weeks in Turin every summer before making our way to Villar Perosa, the family home at the foot of the Alps, in Piedmont. The children and I, together with some of my sisters-in-law and their children, would make our base there from mid-August to the end of September. Gianni would join us for dinner in the evening from his office in Turin, just like the senator, his grandfather, had done so many years before. For all his love of modernity, Gianni had a conservative streak in him. He felt the necessity to preserve old family traditions. And Villar Perosa, a house that had belonged to the Agnellis since the early nineteenth century, was his bridge to a past that had ended abruptly with the death of his parents, who both died at a young age, and the loss of his grandparents shortly after.*

Marella with her children, Edoardo and Margherita, and a family dog.

THE FIRST FEW MONTHS AFTER OUR WED-*ding, I spent hours every day on the sofa, just reading. Now that I no longer had a proper job, life felt like a permanent holiday! Gianni was worried. He could see I had no aptitude for domestic concerns. One day I received a phone call from Contessa Volpi, a Venetian "dragoness" who owned magnificent houses and was known for her savoir faire as a hostess. Gianni had obviously asked her to come to my rescue. "You must come and see me," the old lady roared imperiously into the phone. "I hear that you don't know how to run a home." That's when she told me a hilarious quip I shall never forget: "Remember, my dear girl," she said, "all one needs to catch a husband may be a bed, but it takes a whole house to keep one!"*

Contessa Volpi taught me many things, some more useful than others: how many pairs of sheets one needs for each bed, where to have them embroidered with one's initials, how many porcelain services one needs—things like that. She also gave me counseling on the number of servants needed for each house, where to have their uniforms made, and how to manage their working hours. She taught me the importance of good "placement" for formal dinners and how to create a successful menu.

Contessa Volpi tried to teach me to be parsimonious, something she excelled at. After every dinner she personally smashed all the empty wine bottles. "But why?" I asked naively. "That way," she answered, "staff won't be tempted, at future dinners, to claim that more wine has been consumed than in reality, swindling the extra bottles for themselves."

Marella Agnelli, New York, March 1957. Photograph by CECIL BEATON.

IN THE 1950S OUR LIVES REVOLVED AROUND *a handful of places where a relatively small but international crowd of people would meet. New York was the place to be in November, before the Christmas season. Then there was the skiing season in Saint Moritz, which lasted until March. In summer it was the French Riviera. The summer of 1954, however, we spent in New York, where my son Edoardo was born. He was a beautiful baby and his arrival brought immense joy to our lives.*

Above and opposite: Gianni and Marella sailing in the South of France, mid-1950s, with Edoardo and Margherita. Above photograph by CAMILLA PECCI BLUNT MCGRATH.

Pages 78–79: Gianni and Marella with friends in Séstrieres, an alpine village and ski resort in Piedmont, 1954–55. Photograph by MARINA CICOGNA.

I HAVE ALWAYS LOVED THIS PHOTO OF ME in front of the Orvieto Cathedral, in Umbria, shot by my friend Wanda Gawronska. In it I am wearing a necklace that Gianni gave to me in 1955 during a trip to India with his sister Cristiana and her husband, Brando Brandolini. Gianni, who loved buying jewelry, had scoured the Gem Palace in Jaipur looking for something unique. His eyes had finally stopped on several long strings of rubies and emeralds originally used as a decoration by the maharaja of Jaipur, and he had them restrung as a necklace. In October of that same year, in Lausanne, Switzerland, our daughter Margherita was born. She was a blonde and a delightful child who began to express a talent for painting at a very young age.

Marella, wearing Courrèges, in front of the Orvieto Cathedral, 1955–56. Photograph by WANDA GAWRONSKA.

WHEN WE GOT MARRIED, GIANNI ALREADY owned *La Leopolda, the neo-Palladian villa near the town of Villefranche-sur-Mer, on the French Riviera. It was something out of an F. Scott Fitzgerald novel. Built in the late 1920s by the American architect Ogden Codman Jr. on a property once owned by King Leopold II of Belgium, hence the name, it had become a testament to a collective nostalgia for Belle Époque glamour. Gianni had bought it a couple of years before we got engaged and had asked the French decorator M. Stéphane Boudin to freshen up the* interiors. *Russell Page did some work to the garden. That was all before my time, which is why I never felt a particularly close connection to this property. It belonged to a period of Gianni's life that I had not shared.*

Above: The Agnellis and friends on the terrace of La Leopolda, July 1957. Photograph by BENNO GRAZIANI.

Opposite: Marella and Luciana Pignatelli on the deck of the Agnelli's Chris-Craft in the port of Beaulieu-sur-Mer, 1962. Photograph by HENRY CLARKE.

Page 84: Marella in a gown by Balenciaga, La Leopolda, 1963. Photograph by PHILIPPE HALSMAN.

Page 85: La Leopolda, 1958. Drawing by RENÉ BOUCHÉ.

THE CULTURAL PROMISCUITY OF OUR
small (in terms of number) but cosmopolitan
group heightened our level of interest toward all
things fashionable. People placed great emphasis
on appearance in those days and what one wore
became of extreme importance. Fashion was a
way of expressing oneself and also a defense: if
one wasn't particularly beautiful, and I never
saw myself as a beauty, it was important to at
least be elegant. Mr. Balenciaga, my favorite de-
signer during most of the 1950s, was my shield.
One presented an image invented by someone
else, which was a marvelous feeling.

Pages 86–87: Marella and Gianni with Carlo Caracciolo, far left, and a friend by the swimming pool at La Leopolda, 1957. Photograph by CAMILLA PECCI BLUNT MCGRATH.

Opposite: Portrait of Marella by ERWIN BLUMENFELD.

CORSO MATTEOTTI, TURIN

AND

VILLA BONA, TURIN

AMEDEO ALBERTINI

During the 1960s, the Agnellis divided their time between two homes in Turin that had diametrically opposing visions of architecture and of life. On one hand was the vast opulence of the Agnellis' family residence on Corso Matteotti, in the midst of Turin's historic center. On the other was Villa Bona, a gleaming, high-tech piece of contemporary architecture perched high on the hills overlooking the city.

The palace in Turin had been bought in the early years of the twentieth century by Senatore Giovanni Agnelli, founder of Fiat and Gianni's grandfather. He had envisioned it as the main family residence for generations to come. Gianni and his six siblings grew up there between the two wars. Truman Capote, who stayed there as a houseguest on several occasions in the 1960s—and wrote about it in 1969 for *Vogue*—was taken as much by its "Italian splendor" as by its comforts: " . . . same-day laundry service, buttons everywhere that arouse instant liveried attention, velvet winter rooms ablaze with summer flowers. Pretty nice."

There are few surviving photographs of Corso Matteotti, sadly, but it appears that Marella's décor paid tribute to the previous generations' taste for richly adorned interiors. The rooms, spacious and with high ceilings, were punctuated with fine pieces of Italian Renaissance and Louis XVI fur-

Above: Paintings in Gianni Agnelli's bedroom at Corso Matteotti include works by Francis Bacon, Henry Moore, Alexei Jawlensky, and Emil Nolde. In the salon, Renoir's *La Baigneuse Blonde* hangs over the mantel between Ch'ien Lung porcelain pheasants. Photographs by HORST P. HORST.

Left: Marella, wearing an emerald velvet dress by Dior, in front of a Picasso and an eighteenth-century sculpture of a monkey. Photograph by HENRY CLARKE.

niture. In the living room two Ch'ien Lung porcelain pheasants stood on either side of Renoir's *La Baigneuse Blonde*, dated 1881, which hung over a mirror above the finely carved eighteenth-century marble mantelpiece. Crystal chandeliers descended from the ceiling, heavy brocade curtains draped the windows, and fresh flowers overflowed from large vases.

One of the few signs that this house was lived in by a young, cosmopolitan couple with a taste for modernity was the somewhat subversive presence of modern and contemporary artwork, such as Francis Bacon's 1961 *Studies for a Pope*. A leather sofa in Gianni's bedroom offered an impromptu setting for a movable display of art that included Henry Moore's 1947 *Two Sitting Women* and Emil Nolde's 1915 *Deux Russes*.

Gianni and Marella soon needed more space for their burgeoning art collection. They also, by many accounts, longed for a respite from the hemmed-in formality of the Corso Matteotti home. In 1961 they commissioned Amedeo Albertini (1916–1982), a well-known architect specializing in innovative industrial buildings, to create Villa Bona. This glass-paneled structure, held together by an elegant grid of steel and raw concrete, embodies that era's quest for informality and cultural freedom. The notion of private and public spaces, so intrinsic to Italian culture throughout most of the twentieth century, was overturned in favor of an open space more akin to a residence in Hollywood than in Turin. There are no boundaries or internal walls separating the living from the dining areas or the bar from the breakfast table. Even the bedroom, a freestanding cylindrical structure, was an intrinsic part of the décor. This avant-garde notion included blurring the boundaries between interiors and exteriors, with the heated swimming pool in the living room extending futuristically beyond glass walls and into the garden.

The contradictions between these two opposing visions, the anchored stability of the family residence versus the youthful restlessness that permeates every gleaming inch of Villa Bona, bear testimony to the complexity of Gianni and Marella's quest for an idiosyncratic style that would encompass the past while embracing the future. As an unsigned editorial in the April 1969 issue of *Vogue* put it: "The Agnellis are on-goers, too much in motion, too undogmatic, too interested, too tuned in to be caught by static definitions, although a dramatist, sculptor or social historian determined to pin down a symbol of Italy now would find them irresistible."

BY 1961 GIANNI AND I HAD ACCUMULATED *quite a number of contemporary works of art, but we just didn't know where to put them! This is why we decided to create houses designed specifically around our collection. The first such space was Villa Bona, on the hill overlooking Turin. The minimalist style of its interiors provided the perfect alternative to the more formal environment in Corso Matteotti, in Turin. This was the Agnelli family home, and so when I went to live there after my marriage, I was determined to tread lightly as I knew the house was filled with memories and presences from Gianni's childhood. I didn't want to disturb that. Villa Bona, on the contrary, had been built* ex novo. *It was frontier land, in every sense. I guess it provided that free-spirited lightness that we craved at the time.*

Above: Aerial view of Villa Bona, which is perched on the hills overlooking the city.

Pages 94–95: The swimming pool extends from the outdoor terrace into the living room, which has furniture by Poul Kjærholm and Eero Saarinen. The bronze sculpture to the left is by Fazzini.

Pages 96–97: The living and eating areas open to the outdoors with sliding glass panels; furniture by Mies van der Rohe and Eero Saarinen. The freestanding, curved wood paneling conceals the bedroom area.

Pages 98–99: A view of the cylindrical bedroom at left. The bronze sculpture is by Lynn Chadwick, and the open bar in the foreground is by Gardella.

BRERA APARTMENT, MILAN

GAE AULENTI

"In the 1960s most Italian homes were rigidly traditional and conformist," architect Gae Aulenti (1927–2012) stated in a spring 2012 interview for this book. "Gianni and Marella's houses were different. They were an opening onto the world."

Nowhere is the "world" more present than in the Milan apartment Gianni Agnelli commissioned Aulenti to design in 1969. "We needed to 'invent' an ideal environment, he told me, in which to display his collection of works of art from that decade: Roy Lichtenstein, Francis Bacon, René Magritte, Les Lalannes . . ."

Lighting was to be the leitmotif of this private shrine to the arts. "At that time it was hard to achieve good lighting," Aulenti recalled. "There were museum spotlights or there was traditional home lighting. I wanted to find the balance between direct lighting and diffused lighting." The result of this quest were the apartment's stainless steel cylinder appliqués with hidden spotlights of varying intensity that could be pointed in any direction. To amplify the sensation of diffused lighting, walls and ceilings were covered with an off-white varnish that created a shimmering effect.

Gianni Agnelli had an irreverent streak, Aulenti recalled, that led him to stretch accepted notions of taste to improbable objects. "One day he took me to the Fiat factory in Turin," said the architect. "He wanted to place one of the workshop

Moutons (1966) by François-Xavier Lalanne huddle in the gallery leading to the main living room. On the far wall, Kenneth Noland's *Belix* (1959–60) is visible. All photographs by UGO MULAS.

tables used by mechanical engineers in the center of his living room, right in front of Roy Lichtenstein's 1963 painting *In the Car*. The effect, bizarre as it was, looked amazing." A sense of humor has always been intrinsic to Gianni and Marella's aesthetic, Aulenti continued, as evinced by the presence of a flock of Lalanne "lambs," the translation of *agnelli.*

Marella wasn't much involved at first in the making of this apartment. She regarded it as Gianni's "folly," something he did for his own amusement. It was also good for business: Milan, in those years, promised to become one of the financial centers of the world, and so it seemed vital for the head of Fiat to have a base there. As work on the apartment progressed and became more experimental, Marella began to take a closer look. She was fascinated by the architect's attempts to find a versatile way of lighting the artworks. Aulenti, on the other hand, was impressed with Marella's practical attitude toward interior decoration and design in general: "She kept asking pertinent qutions about every single detail. She kept me, literally, on my toes!"

A friendship blossomed. In the dcades to come, Aulenti and Marella worked together on several projects: two chalets in Saint Moritz, the swimming pool and pavilion in Villar Perosa, and La Petite Maison at Ain Kassimou in Marrakech. Two other Agnelli commissions were a school for the town of Villar Perosa and the restoration of Venice's Palazzo Grassi, which the architect turned into a museum. "In due course I discovered that Marella did not limit herself to the role of Gianni's wife," Aulenti revealed. "She knew how to listen, but at times she could be fiercely headstrong and opinionated."

In the course of her long career, Aulenti went on to design large-scale museum spaces all over the globe: Paris's Musée d'Orsay, Rome's Scuderie del Quirinale, San Francisco's Asian Art Museum, and Barcelona's Museu Nacional d'Art de Catalunya, among others. "In retrospect I would say that what sparked my lifelong interest in the relationship between architecture and art," Gae Aulenti concluded in the interview, one of the last ones before her death in October 2012, "was this long-lost, long-forgotten Milan apartment, which was eventually sold a few years later. It was there that I understood that what matters, when you are confronted by great works of art, is not only what you focus your attention on but also what enters your peripheral vision."

In front of Roy Lichtenstein's *In The Car* (1963) is an industrial table, normally used by Fiat mechanical engineers.

WHENEVER GIANNI AND I WERE IN New York, we spent hours scouring downtown galleries and visiting artists' studios. We were friends with Leo Castelli, who in those years was the eminence of contemporary art in New York City. We soon realized we had no idea where to put the huge works by these young painters we were discovering: Jasper Johns, Robert Rauschenberg, Tom Wesselmann, Frank Stella, Robert Indiana. . . . . So Gianni asked architect Gae Aulenti to design an apartment, in Milan, specifically for this collection. Though it was really Gianni and Gae's project, I became involved in certain aspects of its interior decoration.

Working side by side with Gae, I found myself getting to know her and like her immensely. We were born the same year, 1927. We both enjoyed traveling, reading, and art. What I admired about her was her practical approach to architecture. I remember her telling me once that the most important thing about architecture is not only what it looks like but also how it im-

pacts people's lives. We became friends and many other projects followed that first one in Milan.

During the 1950s and 1960s, Gianni and I would often set up homes in hotels. In Paris it was at The Ritz. In St. Moritz we stayed at the Palace Hotel, and in Rome, for many years, The Grand Hotel.

There were no divisions between the master bedroom and the bathroom, creating one large open space. The bronze sculpture is by Magritte.

THE SIXTIES

IN 1960 I WAS THIRTY-THREE YEARS OLD. *Looking back, I would say that for a woman life only gets better after thirty. The sense of guilt women of my generation tended to have—about traveling, about having fun, about seeing the world, about not being domestic enough—was diminished somewhat by the 1960s. One reason I adored my husband's family was that they projected a liberating feeling that life was there to be enjoyed. But after thirty, in any case, the guilt begins to dissipate.*

In the 1960s, when our children were still young, Gianni used to love to dazzle them with spectacular gestures, such as inviting them to join us for a last-minute trip to The Riviera. We would leave Turin and forty minutes later Gianni and the children would be jumping into the waves straight from a flying helicopter. I didn't enjoy the dives as much as they did, but I joined in so as to not lose face.

Marella, wearing a pale-blue wool Courrèges dress with glittered stockings, in the library at Corso Matteotti, 1967. Photograph by HENRY CLARKE.

GIANNI AND I USED TO TRAVEL A LOT TO *the United States in the 1960s, primarily for Gianni's work as president of Fiat. We had many friends in New York and I felt at home there, partly because I had such good memories of the years I had spent in the city working for Erwin Blumenfeld. At that time, the media started to become more present in our lives. In January of 1960 I had been placed on the* New York Times' *list of best-dressed women, which made me feel honored, of course, but also self-conscious about being suddenly under the spotlight.*

Swan-neck profile in black: Marella Agnelli, New York, December 7, 1959. Photograph by RICHARD AVEDON.

Page 110: Of all the boats Gianni and Marella had in the course of the years, the one Marella still feels most fond of is the *Agneta*, an eighty-foot yacht with dark red sails that made it look especially magestic. They spent many holidays on it in the first half of the 1960s, cruising the Mediterranean with friends and family.

Page 111: This photograph of Marella, taken with infrared film, appeared in *Vogue*, 1961. Photograph by IRVING PENN.

Opposite and above: Marella, Edoardo, and Margherita Agnelli in the 1960s. Photographs of children by MARELLA AGNELLI. Photograph of Marella and her children by CAMILLA PECCI BLUNT MCGRATH.

AFTER JOHN F. KENNEDY BECAME PRESIDENT in 1961, we used to see quite a bit of the Kennedys. I found John charismatic and handsome. John and Gianni shared a passion for yachts and I remember many glorious hours spent with them at sea off the coast of Newport, observing the race between Australia and the United States during the 1962 America's Cup. Gianni was eager for Italy to enter the race as well. He was full of plans and ideas about how to build the perfect racing boat. In the evening, over dinner, we talked about this with John and other friends. Gianni's dream eventually became a reality in 1983, when Azzurra entered the race and came in third.

Opposite: Marella and Jacqueline Kennedy in Amalfi before embarking on the Agnellis' yacht *Agneta*, August 1962.

Above: Gianni and John Kennedy, Newport, Rhode Island, 1962.

115

ONE FRIEND WHO RELISHED BEING PART OF
our summer cruises in the Mediterranean was
Truman Capote. I had met him in New York and
we became friends. Gianni liked him too, finding him amusing and good company. Truman
claimed to love yachting, but he was actually very
lazy and hated anything active like jumping off
boats and going for long swims or sight-seeing.
He had very fair skin and couldn't stand the sun
much, and so he spent a lot of time during the day
in his cabin reading while we all went off to explore the coastline. He would occasionally go for a

swim. Every day he performed some gymnastics
on deck with Gianni. I took some photographs of
them stretching. Truman did everything very
slowly and calmly . . . no rushing around for him.
He didn't like motorboats and speedboats at all.

Pages 116–117, 118–119: Gianni and Marella Agnelli with President and Mrs. Kennedy aboard the United States Coast Guard
yacht *Manitou*, during the America's Cup races, Newport, Rhode
Island, September 1962. Photographs by ROBERT KNUDSEN.

Opposite: Truman Capote and Marella in the sea during a cruise
up the coast of Yugoslavia, August 1966.

Pages 122–123: Gianni and Truman doing morning exercises,
August 1966. Photograph by MARELLA AGNELLI.

IN 1965 TRUMAN JOINED US FOR A BOAT *trip I had organized on the* Sylvia, *a 1956 yacht specifically designed for cruising. We were going to explore the Turkish and Greek coastlines. Gianni, my brother Carlo, my half brother Ettore Rosboch von Wolkenstein, and my young cousin Allegra Caracciolo, who eventually married Gianni's youngest brother, Umberto, were all on board. Katharine Graham, the* Washington Post *publisher, was also there.*

Most of us spent the days swimming and exploring the coastline. Not Truman. Once I said to him, "Truman, you must come with us at least once to see some of the amazing ruins." And he said, "Oh, forget it. One old stone is just like another." He was not interested in sight-seeing whatsoever.

Opposite: Truman in Turkey, summer 1965. Photograph by MARELLA AGNELLI.

Pages 126–133: "The *Sylvia* Odyssey," with photographs and handwritten commentary by Truman Capote, for the January 15, 1966, issue of *Vogue*.

The "Sylvia", a white sailing yacht of grace and speed (seen here anchored in the bay at MYRA, TURKEY), manned by an all-Italian crew of courage and charm. Last summer, when the "Sylvia" spent a month sliding among the Greek islands and along the stark coast of Southern Turkey, most of the passengers were Italian as well, including the hosts of this Elysian adventure, Gianni and Marella Agnelli, and their young son, Edvardo; also Prince Adolfo CARACCIOLO, who was chaperoning his beautiful daughter, Allegra. The other guests were: a gentleman from Copenhagen, Mr. Eric Nielsen; and two Americans: this scribe, and a charming Tycoon from Washington, D.C.;

THE SYLVIA ODYSSEY

Photographs with ∧ (handwritten) Comment

by

TRUMAN CAPOTE

Carlo, a crew-member, looking like a stone head among the stone ruins along lonely Turkish shores.

Mariella, directing a speed-boat into safe-harbor at a Turkish cove where we want to bathe. But, lovely as it was, it turned out not to be too damned safe— a flock of wild bees swarmed out to meet us.

A STOP AT SPETSOPULA

Suddenly, while swimming in the green, ice-clear waters of a Turkish bay near Myra, Kay Graham shouted: "my God! Look! That animal! That octopus!"

Everybody rushed shoreward — except little Eduardo and crew-member Giorgio, who captured the writhing beast, slew him, and, later, sliced, fried, and ate him

— the Greek island privately owned by Stavros Niarchos. Above, Eugenie Niarchos one of a fleet of little al fresco Fiats- used to jaunt about the island's mountainous, pheasant-infested roads, what a place! — for example, There are Two yachts in the harbor: the "CREOLE", that famous black pearl of the Aegean, and the homely "EROS", which is known as "the guests' yacht." Other items: a helicopter-port, from whence you can helihop to Athens in 50 minutes; a Hansel-and-Gretel hunting-lodge hidden high in cool pine-strewn hills; a classic white Greek-island church with windows of pure colored red glass and green glass; a white-sand beach, immaculate as a Japanese rock-garden, and a beach-house complete with Sauna-bath and a jukebox stocked with everything from Bach to 'The Supremes.'

All in all the Niarchos self-made paradise (the island was

On the beach at remote and serene Olympus: a happy Kay Graham, an uninterested camel, and a congregation of friendly and very interested Turkish mountaineers — hard, weathered fellows who fed us delicate cakes, hot mint tea, and, through an interpreter, amused themselves by shyly flirting with the ladies

Foreground: marella.

← Background: a Trout-river
with waterfalls near Side.

↓

Life Aboard SHIP: as the 'Sylvia'
cuts through a moon-bright sea,
marella and Eric Nielsen sip cold
aperitifs while waiting for the Coo
to dish up the pasta (on which I've
gained 6 pounds).

↑ Three generations of a finely-made Italian
family, Right to left: Marella, son Eduardo,
and Marella's elongated, languid, witty
uncle, Prince Adolfo Caracciolo. Someone once
said of Marella: "It took two thousand years
to produce that face." Yet the interesting thing is: her
mother was not Italian, nor even Latin, but

Allegra, sunbathing on a sun-warmed, sea-lapped rock. A true water-nymph — morning or night, her hair was always wet.

Allegra again. A classic girl. These snaps do no justice. None whatever. She is twenty; someone so young seldom possesses mystery. All

Among the Ruins of Turkish OLYMPUS — which are hell to get
to, I might add: one all but CRAWLES through
sweltering Turkish "jungles." Beautiful; but
oh the heat. In desperation, I hurled myself
fully clothed into the depths of this frigid
river (frigid because it is fed by melted
snow sliding down the TAVRUS mountains).

* * *

DURING THE 1960S I REGARDED TRUMAN as one of my closest friends, perhaps the closest. Being warm and amusing, he had the talent to get close and intimate. By the time I met him, I had read his first two books and considered him a young genius. But that wasn't uppermost to me because our relationship, I thought, was based on an elective affinity. I found myself telling him things I never dreamed of telling anyone. He was able to create a deep sense of intimacy. But he was waiting like a falcon.

Very often he would call me and say, "I'm in Verbier and I'm dying of boredom. Can I come visit you in Turin?" There were three or four guest bedrooms, and the one he liked was a large blue room. So when he called he would ask, "Is the blue room empty?" Then he would appear. He never knew exactly how long he was staying or where he was going, and so he arrived with his Louis Vuitton trunks, full of disorder.

THE FIRST TIME I WAS DISAPPOINTED BY Truman—because I thought we had a unique relationship—was at a luncheon he gave at the Colony, the chic restaurant on Madison Avenue. C. Z. Guest was there, Babe Paley was there, and many, many others. We all found ourselves suddenly part of a large group of friends who had more or less the same relationship with Truman. He called us his "swans," but now it seemed there were just too many swans. Some of the swans I didn't even like that much. I had always thought my relationship with Truman was personal. The intimacy, the laughs, the giggles. . . . I thought it was a special friendship between Truman and me, unaware he was also giggling and laughing with Babe or Gloria or Slim. When I told him, "Strange, I thought I was the only swan," he answered only, "Oh, well, darling. . . ."

MY BREAKUP WITH TRUMAN HAPPENED *before the chapter from his novel* Answered Prayers *appeared in* Esquire *magazine in 1975. In this roman à clef Truman exposed the lives and secrets of many people who had regarded him as a close friend and confidant, which is why, when the piece appeared, there was a general uproar. Truman had really gone too far this time, transforming himself from a society darling into a pariah.*

I had tried to warn him on the boat when

he gave me a short section of his book. I can only read English very slowly, and so I asked him to read me a few chapters. What he was writing was very shallow and I remember getting quite cross with him one day, saying, "Oh, Truman, this is a gossip column. What are you getting yourself into?"

AT THAT TIME HE FELT INVINCIBLE. HE

told me he was preparing a Proustian project.

"You must realize," he said, "that I am going to

do to America what Proust did to France." Later,

I often thought that his famous Black and White

Ball, which took place in the Grand Ballroom of

the Plaza Hotel in November 1966, was a way

of gathering together all the characters who were

going to be a part of his novel.

Opposite: Marella and Gianni Agnelli at Truman Capote's Black and White Ball, The Plaza Hotel, New York City, November 28, 1966. Photograph by RAY "SCOTTY" MORRISON.

Pages 138–139: Marella and Gianni, Turin, 1968. Photograph by UGO MULAS.

VIA XXIV MAGGIO APARTMENT, ROME

WARD BENNETT

"This is the only contemporary house I have seen that has true grandeur." Hubert de Givenchy, the French fashion designer and aristocrat, whispered these words in designer Federico Forquet's ear in the early spring of 1970, during one of several house-warming evenings in the Agnellis' Roman residence. The New York–based designer Ward Bennett (1917–2003) had just finished a complete makeover of the apartment and, as Forquet would recall thirty-three years later, the result was causing quite a stir in Rome: "No one in this city had ever made such a defiantly minimalistic interior."

The Agnelli Roman residence occupies the entire fifth floor of a tall nineteenth-century palace on the top of the Quirinal Hill. What attracted Marella and Gianni to it were the monumental proportions of its 1,600-square-foot central living room, with its 26-foot-high ceilings and exaggeratedly tall arched windows commanding dazzling views of the city.

Now the question was who to commission to do the renovations. They found Renzo Mongiardino's plan, based on a patrician house in ancient Rome, too nostalgic. Philip Johnson's super-modern concept with a retractable ceiling proved impossible to get permits for.

This is when Ward Bennett entered the scene. Coincidentally, the New York–based designer had been working for months just two floors below, in the apartment of film producer Roberto Haggiag and his wife, Mirella Petteni. Bennett's style, Marella would recall years later, was restrained and bold. His sleekly designed interiors, combining seemingly incompatible elements, such as Renaissance

Opposite: Entrance hall, lined with large slabs of polished travertine. Isis statue (circa 205–180 B.C.) from Thebes.

Pages 142–143: Entrance hall with Balthus's painting *La Chambre* (1952) and Alberto Giacometti's bronze *L'Objet Invisible* (1934). Photographs by OBERTO GILI.

masterpieces and aboriginal art, suited Gianni's eclectic streak.

Born in Washington Heights, Manhattan, in 1917, Ward Bennett had the experimental versatility of a self-taught designer. After dropping out of school at thirteen to work as a shipping clerk in the garment industry, he traveled to Europe at the age of sixteen, in the 1930s, to learn about art and ended up studying briefly with the sculptor Constantin Brancusi in Paris. In the course of his long career, Bennett tried his hand at window dressing, sculpture, jewelry designing, hat making and, most notably, designing chairs, such as the leather and steel folding chairs in the Agnellis' Roman residence.

This apartment revolves around a long, narrow entrance hall leading to the common areas and private quarters. Lined with large slabs of travertine stone and punctuated by a life-size Egyptian sculpture in black granite, this area's streamlined minimalism—a trademark of Bennett's style—is accentuated by the absence of architectural ornaments, including door and window cornices as well as thresholds.

From this hallway, one accesses the central living room via a tall doorway: the sudden impact of this soaring space, combined with the dizzying views of the city, are made all the more spectacular in contrast to the sober minimalism of the entrance. The focal point, as one enters this room, is provided by a Marino Marini bronze sculpture: a horse and a knight with his head stretched back and his eyes fixed on an invisible point high above. The suspended ceiling, more than thirty feet high, was designed to conceal the spotlights that illuminate the works of art: an Oskar Schlemmer to one side of the room and a Futuristic Giacomo Balla to the other. To the back of the room, Gianni and Marella hung their collection of Robert Indiana numbers in bright red, turquoise, and green. Contemporary art, in the form of murals by Italian Pop artist Mario Schifano, dominates this scene, as well as the dining room. These were commissioned by Marella as a present to Gianni for his fiftieth birthday in 1971.

Marella's unique touch, in this apartment, is in the stark simplicity of the monochrome furnishings: straw mats on the floor, her trademark wicker furniture, and the presence of fresh flowers and potted citrus plants. Off to one side of the living room is the library, a cozy sitting area dedicated to twentieth-century masters, including a painting by Carlo Carrà, a Modigliani nude, and a Constantin Brancusi bronze head. The white-on-white fabric for the curtains of this room is a Federico Forquet design.

Pages 144–145: The main living area with Giacomo Manzù's bronze *La Pattinatrice* (1959) at left and Marino Marini's bronze *Knight and Horse* (1946). Photograph by KAREN RADKAI.

Opposite: Oskar Schlemmer's steel and canvas *Figura* (1921) hangs over the Louis XV mantelpiece. Gustave Moreau's painting *Orestes and the Erinyes* (1891) hangs to the left. Photograph by OBERTO GILI.

EVENTUALLY, IN THE LATE 1960S, WE *decided to buy an apartment in Rome. It was the capital and Gianni had to have a base there. I, too, had my reasons to go: I had lived there after the war and, although my parents were both deceased, my two brothers, Carlo and Nicola, as well as many friends, were living there.*

We settled on a large apartment on the fifth floor of a late nineteenth-century palace, one of the tallest residential buildings in the city. It is right next to the Quirinale, where, before Rome became the capital in 1870, the pope used to reside and which now serves as residence for our head of state.

Page 148: Lucio Fontana's painting *Concetto Spaziale* (1950s) hangs over leather-and-steel stools by Ward Bennett. Photograph by OBERTO GILI.

Page 149: Detail of a tabletop with two Sandro Chia bronze sculptures (1995) and an English armillary sphere (circa 1730). Photograph by OBERTO GILI.

Opposite: The dining area overlooks St. Peter's and Palazzo Colonna garden; chairs by Ward Bennett. Photograph by KAREN RADKAI.

Pages 152–153: Dining room with Mario Schifano murals. Photograph by OBERTO GILI.

INITIALLY, I ASKED RENZO MONGIARDINO to help me. He came up with a good-looking project but it was a little too nostalgic. Rome is the pulsating heart of the ancient world, and both Gianni and I felt we needed something modern, architecturally defiant, to counterbalance the presence of so much antiquity. So we asked Philip Johnson, who came up with an ambitious, futuristic project that revolved around an inner courtyard with a retractable ceiling. The idea was that one could use this space as a living room in winter and as a garden in the summer. But it seemed too complicated to maintain.

In the end we turned to Ward Bennett, a New Yorker who was neither an architect nor a regular interior decorator but who had been the first to introduce industrial materials to home furnishing. We met him through David Rockefeller, and he had been working on Roberto and Mirella Haggiag's apartment two floors below ours. He was self-taught, loved the arts, and had studied briefly under Constantin Brancusi in Paris before the war. This versatility of his attracted me because that is always a sign of an open mind.

Work on the house lasted a couple of years. We gouged out the interiors and rebuilt them anew. Travertine stone—a tribute to Rome's Imperial architecture—lined the entire entrance, from floor to ceiling. We kept everything as streamlined as possible, including the number of rooms. Maintaining a sense of space, dictated by the particularly high ceilings and by the soaring views over the city, was a priority.

Pages 154–155: Library with Amedeo Modigliani's *Nu Couché* (1917). Photograph by KAREN RADKAI.

Opposite: In Marella's bedroom, a portrait of Luisa Casati (1920) by Kees van Dongen hangs over an eighteenth-century white and blue marble mantelpiece. Photograph by OBERTO GILI.

Pages 158–159: Marella's bathroom with marble tub designed by Ward Bennett after a nineteenth-century design. Photograph by KAREN RADKAI.

Pages 160–161: Andy Warhol's *Diamond Dust Shoes* (1980) hangs in Gianni's bedroom. Over the bed is Jim Dine's *Big Black Tie* (circa 1961); Franz Kline's *Suspended* (1953) is to the left. Photographs by OBERTO GILI.

VILLA FRESCOT, TURIN

RENZO MONGIARDINO

From the center of Turin one heads southward along a narrow road that makes its way by twists and turns up a massive hill known as *la collina*. The guarded entrance gate of the Agnellis' private residence, framed by abundant vegetation, is barely visible. Once past the gate, the road winds its way round manicured lawns and past a two-story house that once served as a cowshed and is now covered with ampelopsis vines, before ending on a terraced courtyard leading to the entrance of a compact and solidly built eighteenth-century villa. Villa Frescot, which owes its name to the previous owners, is the setting that sparked the long-lived and fruitful collaboration between architect and designer Renzo Mongiardino (1916–1998) and Marella Agnelli.

When Gianni and Marella acquired this estate in the late 1960s, Frescot's location offered something that the apartment in Corso Matteotti, in the bustling city center, could no longer provide: privacy. It also combined the gracefulness of a storied architecture and the freedom of a rural setting with the comforts of being close to the city. Frescot also had plenty of land on which to create a terraced garden. With the aid of Russell Page and, later, of landscape architect Paolo Pejrone, Marella molded the sloping land into a series of square or rectangular "rooms," all interconnected via staircases and narrow paths and all easily accessible from the house. She went on to plant them with fruit trees, flower borders, and neatly clipped boxwood in the manner of traditional Piedmontese home gardens.

As for the interiors, Marella made a stylistic U-turn from the international modernism that defined other Agnelli projects by summoning Renzo Mongiardino, an architect who proudly placed himself at the opposite spectrum of modern architecture and design.

Opposite: Entrance hall with staircase leading to private quarters. Photograph on Louis XVI bench by Milton Gendel.

Pages 164–165: Albert Gleizes's *Composition* (1939) and Kirsten Pieroth's *Relativity Egg* (2012). Photographs by OBERTO GILI.

Creator of some of the most spectacular interiors of the second half of the twentieth century (his list of clients includes the Onassises, the Brandolinis, the Radziwills, and the Rothschilds, among others), Mongiardino's heart lay in cinema and the theater, where he could unleash his talent for creating highly crafted sets with fantastical references to an idealized past. He was fifty-three years old when Marella summoned him, in the spring of 1969, to see what he could conjure for Villa Frescot. "Renzo was fascinated by the Agnelli aesthetic," Roberto Peregalli, Mongiardino's longtime friend and collaborator, said in the course of a January 2014 interview for this book. "He relished their eclectic pursuit of excellence in all things, whether it was cutlery, porcelain, furniture, or art, and whether it was ancient or contemporary."

That first day on location Marella and Mongiardino spent hours scouring every nook and cranny of the dilapidated house. It was like going on a treasure hunt, Marella recalled years later. The villa had been lived in by the same family for generations and this, together with an obvious lack of financial means, had turned these interiors into a time warp. Though faded and partly destroyed, many of the villa's original nineteenth-century decorative features, such as hand-painted wallpaper, inlaid wooden floors,

bits and pieces of fabric, and most of its original fixtures, were still in place. Frescot was offering this freshly minted team all the clues, as well as the context, to make an imaginative tribute to the rich and varied tradition of Piedmontese arts and crafts.

For months Marella would take daily excursions, camera in hand, to look at historic Piedmontese interiors. She would take in colors and patterns and then, with the help of Mongiardino and his team of craftsmen, elaborate on those inspirations to create a mural decoration, wallpaper, or a fabric. Once Marella went to visit a neighboring villa. "I love your curtains," she told the mistress of the house. "Would you be terribly upset if I send my upholsterer to measure them? I would like to have an identical pair for my dining room."

Mongiardino, as Peregalli recalled, admired Gianni but it was Marella who made the greatest impact on him. The lightness and humor with which she would place very important and sometimes austere pieces, such as Géricault's slave portraits, against a playfully naïve background of delicate colors and flowery patterns delighted him and set the tone for projects to come.

Passage room with Vittorio Bonacina furniture designed by Renzo Mongiardino. All fabric by Marella Agnelli.
Photograph by OBERTO GILI.

THE TUMULTUOUS 1970S COINCIDED WITH several changes in my own life, the most momentous one being the move to a property on the hills overlooking Turin. Villa Frescot marked the starting point of my long collaboration with Renzo Mongiardino, the Italian architect and decorator. Now that my children, Edoardo and Margherita, were young adults, I needed a project and Frescot came to my rescue.

Renzo Mongiardino, an old friend, was a talented visionary. He knew how to infuse a sense of freshness and optimism to timeworn interiors. His nostalgia for the past, which was founded on a deep knowledge of history, never prevented him from conjuring interiors that had a timeless quality about them. That was important to me because I was aware that his version—and our version—of the past was too idealized to be real. It could only make sense if one revived it through an active and vibrant imagination.

Villa Frescot was my bridge into the world of printed fabrics for the home. The fabrics I used in Frescot were custom-made according to my own designs. For inspiration, I scoured archives looking for original eighteenth- and nineteenth-century Piedmontese designs. The result was a range of fabrics reproducing leaves and berries, with their warm, earthy tones on neutral backgrounds.

One day, fashion designer–turned–interior decorator Federico Forquet, an old friend, brought Gustav Zumsteg—the Zurich-based fabric industrialist and pattern maker—to Villa Frescot. What he noticed first as he entered was my fabric prints. He said, "Where do these come from?" When I told him they were mine, he said, "Yes, I know, but where did you buy them?" He couldn't believe that I had had them made specifically for the house. The next thing I knew, I was on a plane to Zurich and about to embark on an unexpected career as a fabric designer. Designing fabric is an ancient craft linked to both art and architecture. It can bring warmth to people's homes, a notion that gave me a sense of purpose. Wealth can make one feel isolated, and so creating this line of fabric and working hard to make it successful made me feel connected.

Opposite: Louis XVI table from 1768 with bronze and porcelain decorations, on which sits a circa-1745 Meissen porcelain monkey.

Pages 170–171: Living room with a pair of eighteenth-century Ch'ien Lung porcelain pheasants and a Wartsky clock. Photographs by OBERTO GILI.

AS FOR THE GARDEN IN FRESCOT, I WANT-ed it to evoke the area's rural traditions. With Russell Page we made a fruit orchard, a kitchen garden filled with aromatic plants, and a cutting garden. We filled borders with different kinds of bulbs and Cape gooseberries, also known as Chinese lantern plants, which open up in autumn into what look like little orange-brown tissue-paper calyxes.

Russell and I worked well together, except when we got into furious fights. Like the one over the horse chestnut trees: there were four of them, enormous, one in each corner, forming a shaded "square" right in front of my studio. One day Russell decided to cut two of them down, just like that, without even telling me! He said they looked crowded.

Frescot became the place where I would go to gather up my energies. After having lived for so many years in the apartment on Corso Matteotti, in the bustling center of Turin, it was marvelous now to walk out of the house and be surrounded by fields and woodland. Being physically removed from the rest of the city gave Gianni and me the opportunity to choose how to divide our time. We could participate to the social goings-on of the city but we could also live a more reserved existence if we needed to.

Opposite: Gateway at the entrance to the gardens. Photograph by FRANÇOIS HALARD

Pages 172–173: Garden room with a pair of large porcelain dogs from the Ch'ien Lung dynasty. Photograph by OBERTO GILI.

Pages 176–177: The terraced gardens of Villa Frescot. Photograph by FRANÇOIS HALARD

CHESA ALCYON, SAINT MORITZ

GAE AULENTI | RENZO MONGIARDINO

Though Gianni and Marella had been frequenting the Engadine valley since the 1950s, staying at the Palace Hotel in Saint Moritz, it was only in the mid-1970s that they decided to find a place of their own. The choice fell on a chalet located on the sunny Suvretta slope just a few miles south of the town center. The chalet was close to the slopes and commanded a bird's-eye view of Lake Maloja. This house, Chesa Alcyon, eventually became Marella's main residence outside of Italy for more than forty years of her life.

Chesa Alcyon had originally been built in 1900 by an Austrian architect. Though the exteriors were well preserved, its interiors had been stripped down to their bones. Marella—who asked Renzo Mongiardino's assistance on this project—needed a basic framework on which to elaborate a decorative narrative. The house's past came to the rescue after the original 1900 architectural drawings were uncovered. This inspired the Marella-Mongiardino team to immerse itself in the style and work of the Viennese Secessionist movement.

In the 1970s, Marella would later recall, it was still possible to find Egon Schiele and Gustav Klimt paintings at relatively reasonable prices. Following the lead of the original Chesa Alcyon, which matched her own tastes, Marella started to follow

Opposite: Living room with Egon Schiele's self-portrait from 1909.

Pages 180–181: Living room with Gustav Klimt's *Sumplandschaft* (1901) over the sofa. All photographs by OBERTO GILI.

the auctions more closely in search of exceptional works by Viennese artists of the period. Among her best finds are a Schiele oil painting, a self-portrait of him naked, as well as a series of rose-garden views by Gustav Klimt. Another favorite of hers were the paintings by Art Nouveau artist Carl Moll.

Mongiardino and Marella designed the main living room and dining room—and the chalet's top floors, where Marella's private quarters were located—around these paintings. Brightly colored geometric and floral patterns, many of them from Marella's line of fabric and others custom-made by Mongiardino's team of Italian craftspeople, complement Klimt's backgrounds. Marella found most of the period furniture in Chesa Alcyon—such as the revolutionary Sitzmachine armchair, designed circa 1908 by Josef Hoffmann, which is in Gianni's studio—in antiques shops and galleries in Vienna and Salzburg. Mongiardino's contribution to these interiors is in the exquisitely designed and executed architectural fixtures—doors, windows, ceilings, railings, wood panels for the walls—all stylistically coherent with the era Marella wanted to evoke.

Something Marella often did in their houses was to create two complementary areas within the same architectural structure, each reflecting the artistic and stylistic preferences of either Gianni or Marella. Nowhere is this juxtaposition more appar-

ent than in Chesa Alcyon. On the top two floors, Marella's *gemütlich* atmosphere, defined by an alluring nostalgia for a bright and colorful pre–World War I era, is counterbalanced by a first floor dominated by Gianni's taste for streamlined, modernist-inspired interiors. Gianni and Marella commissioned Gae Aulenti to design this area. The combination of raw and polished pine surfaces with pale wall-to-wall carpeting provides a neutral background for Gianni's collection of Picasso and Braque drawings. Gae Aulenti's entrance hall, a dramatically dark and long corridor in raw concrete resembling an atomic bunker, is one of the most memorable features of this project. Upon entering it, one was greeted by the framed original Nouveaux Réalistes manifesto, handwritten on a Klein blue piece of paper in Yves Klein's studio in October 1960. In front of it, hanging next to the ski rack, was Tom Wesselman's *Four Roses* collage. Other works in this gallery included an early Andy Warhol oil painting of a Coke bottle, a Robert Rauschenberg assemblage, and a large piece by James Rosenquist.

Opposite: Dining room with Gustav Klimt's *Schloss Kammer Am Attersee* (1910) and varnished wood chairs from the Wiener Werkstätte.

Pages 184–185: Dining room with Gustav Klimt's *Orchard with Rose Bushes* (1911–12) at left and Egon Schiele's *Luisa, Portrait of the Artist's Sister* (circa 1908) at right.

DURING THE LAST FOUR DECADES OF MY *life, Chesa Alcyon became my primary residence. I spent most of my time there surrounded by family and friends. When I wasn't working on fabric collections, I used to go for long walks or on skiing excursions and took care of our Siberian huskies. There I also found ways to indulge the great luxury one never has time for—reading.*

Renzo Mongiardino and I discovered the house had been realized in 1900 by an Austrian architect. This inspired us to create a Viennese Secessionist mood for the interiors. Though considered old-fashioned at the time, Gustav Klimt and Egon Schiele, as well as Carl Moll, were amongst my favorite artists. Luckily, Gianni was happy to indulge my tastes.

This reminds me of the way I found one of the loveliest Klimt paintings I have ever seen: a rose garden. It happened on a ski lift, sitting next to a woman I had never met before. We started to chat, as one does on ski lifts, and I mentioned I was doing up this chalet and that I was being inspired by the Viennese Secessionist movement. The lady told me about an unusual Klimt she

owned, Obstgarten mit Rosen, *and went on to describe it. I got excited because Klimt's garden paintings are rare, and roses have always been my favorite flowers. We did a few slopes together and by the fifth ski-lift ride, the deal was done!*

This particular painting inspired Mongiardino and me to cover the walls of the dining room—where the painting of the rose garden hangs next to Klimt's portrait of his sister—with custom-made geometric fabric using the same shades of blue and green as in the garden painting. Similarly, the pink-and-white cotton stripes for the next-door living room complemented another Klimt painting I have always loved: a nocturnal landscape titled Sumplandschaft.

A corner of an entrance to the living room with Emil Nolde's *Sibirier* (1914) and wicker furniture by Bonacina.

GIANNI ADMIRED MONGIARDINO BUT HE
needed an area of the house to reflect his taste for modernist architecture. We asked Gae Aulenti to design the entire first floor of the chalet, where Gianni's studio and bedroom as well as a large and more formal living room were to be situated. She also designed a futuristic corridor in concrete that looked more like the access to a bunker. Her work was powerful and provided a surprising contrast to the Proustian nostalgia of the interiors I had created with Mongiardino.

I filled the house with potted plants and put freshly cut flowers in all the rooms, like I always do. They immediately make a room come alive. The small wicker baskets that I place in every home looked beautiful in Saint Moritz. Finely woven wicker baskets are one of my secrets: they cost little, look pretty, and are very useful—just right for carrying papers and books.

During the last couple of years, since I no longer can tolerate the altitude of St. Moritz, I have been spending more and more time in Chalet Icy, in Lauenen, Switzerland, which I am slowly renovating. I named it after a husky Gianni and I were particularly fond of.

Opposite: Gae Aulenti's rooms for Gianni Agnelli on the first floor of Chesa Alcyon with Sitzmaschine chair (circa 1904) by Josef Hoffmann.

Page 190: Study with circular table by Aulenti, model of the Agnellis' *Extra Beat* yacht, drawing by Piet Mondrian (1912), and armchair by Josef Hoffmann.

Page 191: Concrete entranceway with Larry Rivers's *Seventy-five Years Later* (1988).

Pages 192–193: Next to skis and boots hangs Tom Wesselmann's *Great American Still Life no. 1* (1962).

THE SEVENTIES

GIANNI AND I CONTINUED TO SPEND SEVERAL *months every winter in New York. In 1972 Andy Warhol did a series of portraits of us. He had asked us to wear black polo-necked sweaters and he took some Polaroids. He was very concentrated and didn't talk much during the shoot.*

Fashion, too, was in a moment of transition. After the rigors of previous decades, one could wear whatever one wanted: a long, flowery skirt one day, a miniskirt the next. My generation had taken fashion a little too seriously, perhaps, and now I would look at my daughter Margherita—who at twenty, in 1976, was married and had her first child—and admire the way she and her friends lived in blue jeans and colorful jumpers. What they did love and take seriously, these younger generations, was their homes. In a way, I became even more interested in decoration, thanks to my daughter.

Opposite: Marella at Villa Bona. Photograph by UGO MULAS.

Pages 196–197: Portraits of Gianni and Marella Agnelli by Andy Warhol, 1972.

Opposite top: Marella with her dogs at Villa Frescot. Photograph by CAMILLA PECCI BLUNT MCGRATH.

Opposite bottom: Marella and her younger brother, Nicola Caracciolo di Castagneto, at Garavicchio, Tuscany, 1975. Photograph by MILTON GENDEL.

Above: Margherita Agnelli with her oldest son, John Elkann, circa 1977. Photograph by PRISCILLA RATTAZZI.

Left: Sixteen-year-old Edoardo Agnelli, 1970. Photograph by MARELLA AGNELLI.

Pages 200–201: Marella and Gianni with their huskies, Turin. Photograph by ENRICA SCALFARI.

NIKI DE SAINT PHALLE AND I FIRST MET IN *Erwin Blumenfeld's studio, in New York. It was in 1952 and Niki, who was three years younger than I, just twenty-two, was married to the American author Harry Mathews. She was extremely pretty and had a natural gracefulness that caught Erwin's eye, which is why he asked her to come and pose for him. Niki and I got on well that day. We went out to nightclubs with friends several times after that but it wasn't until I too got married that our friendship blossomed. It happened in Saint Moritz. In the mid-1950s Gianni and I used to stay at the Palace Hotel while Niki and Harry lived in a beautiful old chalet. They would often invite friends for dinner and, although Niki was a terrible cook, the evenings chez Mathews were great fun because she and Harry surrounded themselves with interesting people. Their house, a lovely old chalet was romantic and extremely untidy.*

Niki has always been attracted, for as long as I can remember, by the idea of magic. She began studying tarot cards at a young age. Over the years she would sometimes offer to read my cards and try to predict my future. Was she good at it? I don't know. All I remember was that she had a contagiously positive outlook. Niki believed—and this was long before the New Age wave—that we are put on this earth for a reason and that life should be lived as an extraordinary journey of spiritual growth and awareness. So whenever a bad or frightening card came up during a reading, she would tell me not to worry, that it was a wonderful opportunity for me to undergo spiritual change and renewal.

One winter day in 1975 in Saint Moritz, Niki, who by now was no longer married to Harry and was a well-known artist, came to see me to talk about a project that, she told me, she had been obsessed with for many years: creating a sculpture garden that would represent the twenty-two major arcana of tarot cards. She told me she had dreamed of this magical garden many years earlier, when she was on her way to recovery from a severe nervous breakdown she had suffered in her late teens. She had been misdiagnosed as a borderline schizophrenic and given electroshock therapy, which was customary at the time in America. Eventually, an enlightened young doctor who believed in the therapeutic effects of artistic self-expression gave Niki some crayons and paper.

This was a major turning point in Niki's life: art became her road out of insanity. Her vivid dream of the tarot garden, she told me that day in Saint Moritz, marked the beginning of her new life as an artist. The time had now come, she told me, to make that dream a reality. She was a well-known artist by then and she could afford to put her energy and finances into this ambitious project that she regarded as her masterpiece. The question now was no longer "when" to make it but "where"! She longed for it to be in Italy, the country that symbolized art itself.

My immediate response to her was, "Why not do it in Garavicchio?" This is a property in southern Tuscany that my father had bought in 1960 and which now belonged to my brothers, Carlo and Nicola. Niki was delighted at this prospect so I organized her first visit to see the estate and meet my brothers. She arrived all dressed up in a colorful robe topped by one of her

magnificent wide-brimmed hats. The artist Jean Tinguely, who had been the love of Niki's life for many years and was still her artistic partner, was there too.

Niki arrived in Garavicchio that day with a handmade clay maquette of the tarot garden. It looked tiny and totally harmless. My brothers and my sister-in-law Rossella, Nicola's wife, were charmed by her and agreed to give her a piece of their land. There was a natural amphitheater immersed in vegetation and which some two thousand years earlier had been used as a burial ground by the Etruscans. Niki loved this connection with a past civilization she admired. So that's how the Tarot Garden, a garden I did not make myself but that I still feel very close to, came to be.

Pages 202–203: View of Niki de Saint Phalle's Tarot Garden in Garavicchio, the Caracciolo family estate, Tuscany, circa 2005.

Pages 206–207: Examples of the dozens of colorfully illustrated letters that Niki de Saint Phalle sent to Marella and Gianni; details of the Tarot Garden in Garavicchio. Photographs by ALEXANDRE BAILHACHE.

770 PARK AVENUE, NEW YORK CITY

RENZO MONGIARDINO | PETER MARINO

Gianni and Marella Agnelli began to develop strong cultural and social connections in New York in the 1950s but it was not until the mid-1970s that they bought their first apartment there, at 720 Park Avenue. Though relatively compact, this well-proportioned space had the added attraction, in Gianni and Marella's eyes, of having been designed in the 1920s by Rosario Candela, the Italian-American architect renowned for his highly wrought, superbly laid-out Upper East Side luxury buildings. But by 1981 it became clear that the apartment, which had been "done up" by Marella and her decorator friend Françoise de la Renta, was too small to contain the Agnellis' expanding collection of art.

They settled for a larger apartment in another Candela building down the road, at 770 Park. If the earlier apartment had been a decorative divertissement for Marella—Françoise and she had experimented with an eclectic mix of patterns—this time Gianni wanted a full-blown refurbishment.

The two people Marella turned to for this project couldn't have been more different. On the one hand was Renzo Mongiardino, who by now had an intuitive affinity for Marella's taste. On the other was a young Italian-American architect, Peter Marino, whom Marella had met through her daughter, Margherita. A lot has been said about which of the

A Picasso painting of a harlequin from 1909 over a Russian neo-classical ormolu and red quartzite table in the entrance hall. All photographs by ERIC BOMAN.

two designers did what and where in the apartment—and about the supposed tensions between the elderly, aristocratic Mongiardino and Peter Marino, a self-described "working-class Neapolitan kid from Brooklyn with a horrible Italian accent," who was a rising star in the landscape of contemporary interior design in New York.

Although the situation was potentially explosive, as Marella herself later admitted, the reality of it was much simpler because the two architects she commissioned had distinct roles and met each other as few times as possible. "The thing that struck me most about Marella," Peter Marino recalled in an interview for this book that took place at his New York office in December 2013, "was what a great manager of people she was. The best advice she ever gave me was, "Don't try to put a square person in a circle, it just won't work." She looked at three apartments I had done: she opened drawers, checked hinges, examined every detail, and took notes before deciding to take me on board."

Marella decided that Renzo Mongiardino, who was based in Milan and disliked traveling, should conjure spectacular settings for the three main rooms—living, dining, and library—and for the hallway. Peter Marino, who at the time already employed nearly twenty people, was commissioned to supervise the making of these rooms as well as to design the other areas of the house, including Gianni and Marella's private quarters, the breakfast room, and the kitchen.

The Agnellis' artworks offered the decorative leitmotif of these interiors. The Matisse paintings in the living room inspired Mongiardino to juxtapose a mix of geometric print fabrics—white-and-blue stripes for the wall, a bright red-and-white crisscross pattern for the curtains—for the similar effect. Bright-red velvet sofas, including a couple of love seats, paid tribute to the pre–World War I Belle Époque feel of this room's artwork. A different mood was established in the living room, where a collection of eighteenth-century green-and-gold-plated porcelain plates from Imperial Russia inspired Mongiardino to create a custom-made hand-painted wallpaper reproducing some of the floral decoration on the plates. Two large 1750s views of Dresden by Bernardo Bellotto completed the scene, while the small red-lacquer entrance hall was dominated by the imposing presence of a Picasso harlequin portrait.

Pages 210–211: Living room with Balthus painting *Le chat de la mediterranée* (circa 1949).

Pages 212–213: Dining room with mid–nineteenth-century porcelain plates from the Russian imperial collection and Russian neoclassical chairs (circa 1790).

Opposite: View from the dining room into the breakfast room where paintings by Carlo Bossoli cover the walls.

A Tamara de Lempicka portrait of a man who looked uncannily like Gianni when he was young was placed by Peter Marino at the end of a corridor leading to Gianni and Marella's private quarters. An Ignacio Zuloaga painting of a naked woman on a sofa, which is now in one of Marella's living rooms in Marrakech, hung above Gianni's bedroom sofa, while a Louis XVI desk, a masterpiece of its kind, dominated his studio. Peter Marino also designed Marella's quarters on the top floor.

"Gianni would take me to art galleries on Saturday mornings. He looked for things that were unique and unpredictable, never mainstream," Marino recalls. As for Marella, the architect recalls that she, "with her magic wand," opened up the world of Europe to him and introduced him to Diana Vreeland. "She even corrected my Italian. 'Peterino'—that's how she would call me—'you must get rid of your slang, brush up on your Tuscan accent!'" Marino muses on what he describes as Marella's aesthetic intuition. "I remember once trying thirty different lamps for the living room and getting so frustrated until she arrived and immediately picked the right one. It was perfect. She was professional and did not tolerate people being late. It happened to me once and I nearly got sacked on the spot. Needless to say it never happened again."

The New York apartment was sold in October 2004, less than ten months after Gianni Agnelli's death. Many of the paintings it hosted are now in the Pinacoteca Gianni e Marella Agnelli, the museum space designed by Renzo Piano that stands on top of the Lingotto, the Fiat headquarters, in Turin.

Corridor leading from the entrance hall to the private quarters, with Tamara de Lempicka's portrait of Marquis d'Affitto (circa 1925) on the far wall.

NEW YORK WAS THE PLACE WHERE GIANNI *and I pursued our interest in art. In 1980 Gianni decided we needed a place in New York where we could put our collection and so we moved into an apartment at 770 Park Avenue.*

My first choice to help me "do up" this home was Renzo Mongiardino, whose vision—especially after the work we did together in Turin and Saint Moritz—I trusted absolutely. But Renzo, who was well into his sixties by then, was based in Milan and disliked traveling. Although he happily accepted the commission of decorating the apartment's main rooms—namely the entrance hall, the living room, the library, and the dining room—we both agreed that we would need an architect in New York to get it all done. This wasn't an easy feat. I wanted someone who could help with all the paperwork but who was also sensitive and intelligent enough to translate Renzo's and my ideas into reality. He would have to do a great job on the rest of the apartment, too.

Pages 218–219: Marella's bedroom with cream-and-blue painted Louis XVI bed. At the dressing table is a pink-upholstered *coiffeuse* (circa 1750).

Opposite: Adjoining bathroom, designed by Peter Marino.

AFTER SOME RESEARCH, MY CHOICE FELL ON architect and decorator Peter Marino, who was then in his early thirties. Peterino, as I called him, was a friend of my daughter's and of her then-husband Alain Elkann, and so that's how we first met. Despite his young age, Peter was establishing himself quickly in New York. After seeing some of his projects in the city, especially Andy Warhol's Factory and the apartment for Yves Saint Laurent and Pierre Bergé, I knew he was the person for the job.

Mongiardino and I spent many hours imagining the most interesting ways in which we could create a unique setting for the art. The decoration of the living room, with its bright-red velvet sofas against blue-and-white striped walls and checkered curtains, revolved entirely around a series of paintings by Matisse and a wonderfully surreal Balthus painting of a cat dressed up and eating a fish under a rainbow. Similarly, what set the tone of the dining room—the walls of which had been covered with an old wallpaper—was a collection of porcelain plates from Imperial Russia.

What fascinated me most about doing up a home in Manhattan was having to readjust mentally to a notion of space that was much more limited than the one I was used to. Here, more than anywhere else I know in the world, the efficient use of space is essential. It is a place where every single centimeter of closet space has to be mapped out and where the width of every door must be brought down to a minimum. Peter Marino was very good at these made-to-measure calculations and, in the end, our apartment felt more like a sleek yacht than a home. Life moves faster in New York, and so this was the perfect place for me, where I could meet the demands of my busy schedule with maximum efficiency.

Opposite: Gianni's study with Aristide Maillol's sculpture of a torso from 1921 on an ormolu-mounted Louis XVI table.

Pages 224–225: Study with painting, on right, by Alexandre-Romain Honnet.

Pages 226–227: Gianni's bedroom with a Russian neoclassical desk (circa 1805).

THE EIGHTIES

DURING THE 1980S GIANNI AND I FOUND *ourselves spending more and more time in New York City. This was partly because of business and partly because Manhattan, in the late 1970s and throughout the 1980s, was far more cultivated than anywhere else in Europe. The reason for this, I think, was that New Yorkers had made a significant cultural choice: art, filmmaking, and literature were deemed of vital importance. Extravagant amounts of money were being spent on culture—and the flow of money inevitably brings talent and ideas to the surface. The* New York Review of Books, *for example, could only have survived in New York and yet I don't know one writer in Europe who wouldn't have wanted to write for that publication. If something interesting was going on in the world, it was in New York.*

Opposite: Marella Agnelli with her dogs, Turin. Photograph by FRANCO CALOSSO

Pages 230–231: Gianni Agnelli with one of his dogs, Turin. Photograph by PRISCILLA RATTAZZI.

EVERY TIME I PLAN A GARDEN, I ASK MYSELF the same question: how are we going to live in it? In my view, and perhaps it is an exceedingly practical one, gardens are borne out of necessity. How does one live in a garden? How does one want to spend one's time there? Will one need shelter from the sun or from the wind? Will one want a place in which to sit and contemplate the view, or to read? And if it is exceedingly hot, is there a place to swim? These are just a few of the questions I ask myself when I think about making a garden.

In Villar Perosa, where I spent one month every summer since my marriage to Gianni in 1953, the days were passed reading, tending the garden, and taking long walks in the mountains. There wasn't much for children to do, apart from running up and down the garden. Which is why, in the early 1990s, much to the delight of my eight grandchildren, Margherita's children, I decided to build a swimming pool at the foot of the garden.

Gianni was not happy with the idea. Having spent so much of his own childhood here, he didn't like the idea of change.

I went ahead and asked Gae Aulenti to plan a swimming pool area and pavilion that even Gianni would end up loving. We needed to find a way, I told her, for the pool to reflect the greens and grays of the surrounding forest. Gae said the only way to achieve the color I wanted was to line the pool with bright orange cotto tiles. Once it was filled with water, she assured me, it would turn green. One day Gianni and I went to Villar with Gae to check the building site. I remember looking down from the helicopter and, much to our dismay, the bright-orange pool—long and narrow and still empty, for the time being, of water—looked like a huge carrot! Gianni's icy silence fell upon the three of us. When we finally filled the pool, a few weeks later, the carrot turned to a most restful tone of green. Gianni saw it first and phoned *me to give me the good news. Just the color we had wanted. Gae had been right. What a relief!*

Gae, who admired Japanese culture, designed a wooden pavilion next to the pool from large tree trunks—all local plants, pines, and larches—in the manner of traditional Japanese architecture. Besides a changing area, with a sauna, the pavilion has a large living room, a dining area, and a kitchen. When the weather is good, that is where we have lunch. As for the garden surrounding the pavilion, Gianni and I decided it had to be different from the more classical structure of other areas, which is why we decided to place some twentieth-century statues in this part, including a René Magritte torso, a Henry Moore, and a César. With Paolo Pejrone, we planted wild grasses, roses, and a hedge of boxwood that runs along one side of the pool. We covered the sloping hill leading to the pavilion and pool with heather.

Before the swimming pool was built, no one would ever come to this part of the garden. Now this area has become a vital space for all of us, from the youngest to the oldest members of the family. I am always fascinated by the way architecture and gardens influence the way we live our daily lives. This, to me, is one of the wonders of architecture and landscaping: their influence on our personal lifestyle and affections.

Pages 232–233: View of the pool pavilion as one arrives from the villa, with César's sculpture *La Victoire de Villetaneuse* (1965) in the foreground.

Pages 236–237: View of the pool, surrounded by both stylized and natural plantings. Photographs by OBERTO GILI.

"IL CONVENTO," ALZIPRATU, CORSICA

The sixteenth-century convent of Alzipratu is nestled in a valley in the region of Balagne, northwestern Corsica. Built in 1509 as a spiritual and farming retreat for monks, its austere grandeur echoes the rugged wilderness of the surrounding mountains. Less than eleven miles away and in full view from the convent's terrace is the ocean.

This closeness to the sea, and to the port town of Calvi, is what induced the Agnellis, in the mid-1970s, to rent "*il convento*" (as they called it) as a summer retreat. By then the French Riviera had become too crowded for their taste. Corsica, with its windswept coastlines and Mediterranean climate, provided the perfect alternative for Gianni's sailing adventures. In 1989 the convent's longtime French owner, Baron Henry-Louis de La Grange, a musicologist and Gustav Mahler connoisseur, announced he was going to sell. Gianni, who had grown fond of the place, bought it and presented it to Marella as a fait accompli—just in time for a thorough makeover.

The shell of the building, with its thick walls, high vaulted ceilings (some of them retaining fragments of frescos), and original cotto flooring, had a patina Marella wanted to preserve. She focused on comfort by creating extra bathrooms, building a proper kitchen, and updating the electrical system. She then proceeded to lighten up the convent's

View of the estate. All photographs by FRANÇOIS HALARD.

somewhat gothic atmosphere by replacing the baron's heavy-seeming décor, mostly nineteenth-century reproductions of early Renaissance pieces, with graceful Louis XV and Louis XVI French furniture. The best catch, she later recalled, was laying her hands on a collection of French eighteenth-century beds, each one with its own original toile de Jouy fabric. Personal objects were brought in, including a 1946 portrait of the old Senatore Agnelli, which was placed on the mantelpiece in Gianni's bedroom, and a collection of framed dried-flower compositions by Stuart Thornton, the family's longtime butler. Other familiar touches were Marella's fabric designs, such as the deep green-and-pink floral print in the "music room" and her favorite wicker furniture.

The garden posed greater challenges. The grounds had been transformed by the baron into an open-air concert hall with cemented paths and paved areas for the audience to sit in. Architect Paolo Pejrone, who had been working with Marella on the gardens of Villar Perosa and Frescot, came to the rescue. "We tore through the convent's grounds," Pejrone recalled during an interview for this book in November 2013, "eradicating concrete pergolas, paved surfaces, and the swimming pool area. The day after the workmen and their bulldozers finally left, the place was a mess. I said to Marella: 'Why don't we gather the boat crew and all the house staff—the cooks, the English butler, and the housemaids—to help clean up the garden?' So that's what happened. Marella and I—each of us carrying rubbish bags in our hands—joined the team."

The garden of Alzipratu, as Marella and Paolo Pejrone planned it, is in fact two adjoining gardens offering diametrically opposed experiences. On the one hand, facing north, is a cloistered area enclosed by the L-shape of the convent and the church. Jasmine and 'Star of India' clematis cover the walls and a thickly planted citrus grove encloses the area from the other two sides. A round fountain, home to croaking frogs and water lilies, sits at the center of this cloister, underlining its quietly contemplative atmosphere. A few steps past the convent and one suddenly steps onto a grassy plateau that opens onto dramatic vistas over the valley, the mountains, and the ocean below. The greatest challenge of all was to mold the sloping land of this area into a series of terraced gardens sustained by rows of handmade dry stone walls and by thousands of aromatic plants brought in from nurseries all over Italy. With the help of head gardener Thierry Fuentes, a cutting garden, an orchard, and a vegetable plot were planted on these terraces. As gardeners working for Marella have long known, these "domestic" areas have always been central to the experience—and aesthetic—of all the Agnelli gardens.

Detail of the garden with hydrangea bushes and ampelopsis-covered walls.

FOR YEARS—STARTING IN THE EARLY 1970S— Gianni and I used to rent "il convento," as we always called it, from a Frenchman, Henry-Louis de La Grange, one of the world's greatest experts on Gustav Mahler, who had transformed the grounds of this ancient convent on the island of Corsica into an open-air concert hall that hosted a yearly music festival. All around the house was a grid of cement paths and seating areas for the audience. The garden area was kept to a bare minimum, which is why I wasn't so fond of this place initially.

Gianni, however, absolutely loved this place. He adored the rugged beauty of the landscape as much as its closeness to the sea, with those strong Corsican winds that provide excellent sailing conditions. He would come and sail here whenever he could. By then the Côte d'Azur was over—out-of-date and overcrowded. Corsica was a perfect alternative to it.

One day during the winter of 1989, Gianni surprised me. "I bought the convent!" he said gleefully. I was horrified. The last thing I needed at that time was to be saddled with that dreary old place in the middle of nowhere.

But I freshened it up with paint, built more bathrooms and quarters for the staff, and created a large, comfortable kitchen. The proportions of the convent, with its vaulted rooms, were balanced and harmonious and so there wasn't much to do from an architectural point of view. I used mostly eighteenth-century furniture, some of which I bought at auction.

Opposite: The entrance gallery of the convent.

Pages 244–245: The music room has wicker chairs by Res Nova, Turin, and an eighteenth-century Venetian walnut table. Marella Agnelli designed the green-and-pink floral fabric on the walls, curtains, and furniture.

Pages 246–247: Main living room, with a collection of mid-nineteenth-century prints from Edward Lear's *Parrots* series, needlepoint-covered Empire sofa and armchair, and early nineteenth-century tufted armchairs covered in vintage red linen.

FOR THE GARDEN I ASKED GARDEN ARCHI-
tect Paolo Pejrone, a friend and a superb gardener with impressive botanical knowledge, to give
me a hand. After Russell Page's death, Paolo was
the one who had helped me with the gardens of
Frescot and Villar Perosa. We tore through the
garden, erasing all the paved surfaces, the ghastly
pergolas, and even the old swimming pool area.
We planted a potager, which became, in time, the
heart of the garden.

The greatest challenge of all, as far as the
garden was concerned, was to mold the sloping
land into a series of terraced gardens. I remember the long hours spent with Paolo, poring over
nursery catalogs and writing long lists of plants
to be delivered to the convent. What fun we had
planning it all, and what hard work it was to
get it all done!

When he sneakily bought il convento
without telling me, Gianni was sure I would
eventually learn to love it. He was right. The
complete enjoyment I experienced restoring its
interiors and planting a garden around it will
always be a special part of my life.

Pages 248–249: Guest bedroom with bed canopied in
eighteenth-century toile de Jouy, part of a collection that
Marella bought for the house.

Page 250: Framed dried flowers from the various Agnelli gardens,
by Stuart Thornton.

Page 251: Guest bedroom.

Opposite: The patio, covered by a thatched canopy, is surrounded
by ivy and cypresses.

Pages 254–255: From the cutting garden, with rosebushes and
olive trees, views of the mountains of Corsica and the village of
Montegrosso.

THE NINETIES TO THE PRESENT

LOOKING BACK, I WOULD SAY THE 1990S WERE *a happy decade for us, filled with house and garden projects, work, and travel. For my book of photographs on Italian villas and gardens, I traveled all over the country in search of the most beautiful examples of these. I felt it was important to show the world the diversity and beauty of my country. After that I did a book on Ninfa, an extraordinarily beautiful garden on the Pontine Plain, south of Rome. It was created by three generations of women belonging to the princely Caetani family. Now that it belongs to the Fondazione Roffredo Caetani, it is open to the public.*

Gianni and Marella Agnelli, Turin. Photograph by CAMILLA PECCI BLUNT MCGRATH.

THE BEGINNING OF THE NEW CENTURY

brought unexpected sorrows in my life and in that of my family. First was the death of my son, Edoardo, in November 2000. This was followed two years later by Gianni's demise in January 2003. Painful family vicissitudes followed.

Pages 258–259: Gianni and Marella with family, Villar Perosa.

Above: Edoardo Agnelli.

Opposite: Gianni and Marella, Villar Perosa.

AIN KASSIMOU, MARRAKECH

GAE AULENTI | MADISON COX | ALBERTO PINTO

Marella Agnelli's sixty-four-acre property just north of Marrakech owes its name to three underground streams that intersect right there, in Ain Kassimou—the "eye of the source" in Berber dialect. Tall walls covered with jasmine and roses separate the estate from the surrounding *palmeraie*, infusing an aura of remoteness to it. Once inside, past the entrance gates overgrown with bougainvillea and beyond a long allée of cypress trees, is Marella Agnelli's last, wildly ambitious project, one she embarked on at the grand age of seventy-six.

This story began in the fall of 2003, three years after the death of her only son, Edoardo, and a few months after Gianni's death. Architect Gae Aulenti and designer Federico Forquet, two of Marella's closest friends, urged her to make a radical change. Forquet, a passionate gardener and interior decorator, recalled in an interview for this book that Gae and he understood that what Marella needed at that point in her life was a project. "Something exceptional that would rekindle her creative energy and help her survive these tragic losses." Marella agreed. As long as she could find something on a large-enough scale to become a full-time project, and as long as it was in a warm, dry climate, she was ready to take on a new adventure.

Opposite: One of many rustic pergolas (their combined length on the property covers one kilometer).

Pages 264–265: View across a Madison Cox–designed pond, with different varieties of water lilies and papyrus, to the pool pavilion. Photographs by OBERTO GILI.

Ain Kassimou, a property she and Gianni had occasionally rented for winter breaks, came up for sale. Marella seized the opportunity. She relished the remoteness of its location. Although it didn't have a garden, only barren polo fields, Marella recalled being charmed by the main house, a one-story building immersed in olive and citrus groves that was—and still is—named after Count Tolstoy, one of the writer's sons, who took refuge here after the Russian Revolution. Gae Aulenti was commissioned to consolidate the property's main buildings and to help create a guesthouse at the end of the garden.

As for the interiors, Ain Kassimou became an opportunity for Marella to explore Morocco's rich and varied arts-and-crafts traditions while pursuing her lifelong quest for finely crafted natural materials. Paris-based designer Alberto Pinto (1943–2012), a native Moroccan from Casablanca and internationally acclaimed for his exquisitely executed grand-scale projects, became her guide. Walls and ceilings were covered with painted majolicas, embossed stucco, wood carvings, or painted decorations; straw matting and Berber rugs, as well as ancient embroideries, were individually chosen by Marella. "Most of my clients avoid the pains-

A native 'Beldi' rose against a traditional Moroccan pisé wall made of compact earth. Photograph by OBERTO GILI.

taking process of putting a house together," Pinto stated during a conversation that took place in May 2012 at his apartment at the hotel La Mamounia in Marrakech. "Marella is different: she is inquisitive, curious, and pays attention to every single detail. I have never learned so much from anyone as I have from her."

The mentor who guided Marella through the unchartered territory of creating a garden in this oasis in the desert was American garden designer Madison Cox, the longtime curator of the Jardin Majorelles in Marrakech and an expert with firsthand experience on cultivating gardens in the Maghreb. "The first thing I did was to get Marella acquainted with the plants of North Africa," Cox recalled in the fall of 2013 during a conversation for this book. "We visited innumerable gardens and nurseries all over Europe and Morocco and consulted dozens of books." Their common aim, he said, was to create something in the tradition of the classic *jardin des delices*, but first it was necessary to impose structure. "It was haphazard and overgrown," Cox told Hamish Bowles during a 2006 interview for *Vogue*. "I just started clearing things away. We started to reveal the old bones that were there in the era of Tolstoy's son." This garden was created in a spirit of urgency. Marella had no time to wait around for it to grow into place. Two freight containers filled with plants—including centuries-old olive trees—made their way to Marrakech from nurseries in Italy, Spain, France, and England. Other specimens were found locally. Fountains, channels of water, a swimming pool, and ponds were built. Cox commissioned Moroccan-based designer Bill Willis (1937–2009) to create a pavilion specifically for this garden. All in all, more than a hundred people, including thirty-six gardeners from the nearby village, who continue to work at Ain Kassimou full-time, worked on this garden project for two years.

Creating this garden turned out to be a tremendous challenge for everyone involved. "It will probably be unique in my career," Cox told *Vogue*. "Because one could never replicate it." What he learned from Marella, he added, was not to be afraid to be simple and to enjoy every stage in the gardening process. "I think the number-one thing I've learned from her, even beyond the little tricks of the trade, is to have the courage and energy to take on a project of that scale—at her age, when most people are thinking of simplifying and downsizing. She was determined to make this venture work, and she believed in all of us. That is an amazing lesson."

"What Marella wanted to achieve at Ain Kassimou," Gae Aulenti concluded in an interview for this book, "was a synergy in which isolated elements of Moroccan architecture were placed in a context defined by her own cultural and aesthetic sensibilities. I have never met anyone," she added, "who knows how to infuse life into places the way she does. It's as if she has a sixth sense that allows her to see into the future of how a place will become."

Opposite: South-facing façade of the main house, covered in bougainvillea, mermaid roses, and jasmine. Moroccan trelliswork covers the living room windows, 2006.

Pages 270–271: The sitting room with wicker chairs designed by Gae Aulenti for Vittorio Bonacina. The chromolithographs are from a series of Alupka scenes by Carlo Bossoli (1842–43), 2006. Photographs by ERIC BOMAN.

BACK IN THE 1980S GIANNI AND I USED TO *sometimes rent this property, just outside of Marrakech, for mid-winter breaks. The house had been built by a son of Tolstoy's in the 1920s. It had charm but it was small. Though I loved the climate, the grounds—filled as they were with polo fields and paddocks—were not to my taste. The garden was tiny and overgrown.*

In late 2003, when I was looking for a place in a warm climate where I could create a garden, I found out that Ain Kassimou was up for sale. This project required a lot of time, a lot of energy, and a lot of traveling away from home. Like at other times in my life, I made an instinctive decision and went ahead with it. After all, I love this country, with its blazing light and dry climate, and I like its people. I was also taken by the idea of creating a garden from scratch in a territory I was not acquainted with.

Opposite: Entrance hall with walls covered in traditional woven straw made on the property by Moroccan craftspeople. Michelangelo Pistoletto's *Giaguaro in Gabbia* hangs on the wall behind the collection of ancient glass carafes from Syria, 2006.

Pages 274–275: Living room with a selection from *Parrots* (1832), a collection of hand-painted lithographs by Edward Lear. Photographs by ERIC BOMAN.

Page 276: Roses from the garden.

Page 277: *Reclining Maja with Blue and Gold Parrot* by Ignacio Zuloaga y Zabaleta hangs over a table in the living room. Photographs by OBERTO GILI.

WHEN IN LATE 2003 I FIRST ANNOUNCED *that I had my eye on a property in Morocco and that the making of it would occupy my time and energies for years to come, some of my friends and family members thought I was doing a folly. "Why go so far away from home?" they said. "It needs so much work and you are not used to that climate—you will melt away under that African sun!" They were worried for me but I knew this project was going to bring me a lot of comfort and joy—and them, too—in the long run. My granddaughter Ginevra got married here to Giovanni Gaetani dell'Aquila d'Aragona and my grandchildren and great-grandchildren often come to visit.*

Gae Aulenti, a close friend and architect whose work Gianni and I have always admired, was one of the people who backed me up on this Moroccan enterprise. When I told her my worries about getting it done in time to enjoy it, she said, "Of course we'll get it done!" She was right. With her help we enlarged the buildings and made them more stable. This project, which became the beautiful Ain Kassimou, turned out to be far more challenging than expected. The tall building was so damp and brittle it could hardly stand up. I remember we made a hole to build a fireplace and the whole wall came crumbling down.

Pages 278–279: Marella's bedroom has a bed with an Italian lace canopy and Gae Aulenti–designed wicker chairs.

Pages 280–281: Marella's study on the top floor. Morning glories were grown in the property's greenhouse.

Opposite: Outside the main house, a fountain made of marble from a quarry in northern Morocco is surrounded by myrtle bushes.

Page 284: Garden path leading to a side entrance of the main villa through espaliered lemon trees, 2006. Photographs by ERIC BOMAN.

Page 285: A Moroccan desert dog, one of several rescued by Marella and living on the property, 2010. Photograph by OBERTO GILI.

THE PERSON WHO HELPED ME REALIZE THIS

garden is Madison Cox, an American garden designer who spends many months a year living and working in Morocco. I knew and admired his work and trusted his knowledge of the territory. Together we toured local gardens and looked at nurseries of African plants.

In Corsica I had an excellent head gardener, Thierry Fuentes. When I came to Morocco, I asked him to join me. He came to live here full-time with his wife and small children. Under Madison's guidance, he taught the local gardeners to work as a team. He also makes stunning floral arrangements for the house, mixing flowers, wild herbs, and foliage. I like my houses filled with fresh flowers and have a different flower arrangement for the table at every meal.

Opposite: The vegetable garden in the olive grove, with cardoon in the foreground.

Pages 288–289: One of many rustic pergolas (their combined length on the property covers one kilometer) bordered by nasturtiums and cacti. Photographs by OBERTO GILI.

SOME PEOPLE LIKE TO LOOK AT GARDENS. I *love to live them. Every day, when I am in Ain Kassimou, I go for long walks. There are shaded paths and sitting areas scattered all over the property. In the daytime, we often eat outside, under the pavilion that designer Bill Willis, a friend of Madison's who was based in Marrakech for most of his life, created specifically for this garden. It stands next to a pond filled with fish and frogs. This garden has many surprises: pools and streams of rippling water, a rose garden. Thousands of roses, some three hundred different varieties, were planted. My favorites are 'New Dawn' and a very pretty, leafy local rose called 'Beldi,' which smells delicious. There is also an area for succulent plants, an orchard, and a vegetable garden. Morocco, as Madison tells me, is a cold country with a very hot sun. Ain Kassimou offers respite from it.*

Opposite: Detail of a pergola made with bamboo and eucalyptus branches tied together with palm fronds.

Pages 292–293: Wild delphiniums growing under Kashmir cypress trees and next to a traditional Moroccan structure used for growing table grapes. Photographs by OBERTO GILI.

AN OLD FAMILY FRIEND, SANDRO D'URSO,
*used to say to me, "Why make one's dreams come
true when the best part of any project is just
dreaming about it?" He was right, of course,
when it comes to making a house or writing a
book. But with gardens it is different. And like
all living things, they grow and change. That is
a fascinating process to experience.*

Left: Donkeys outside the walled garden in the olive grove.

Pages 296–297: Square pool designed by Madison Cox. The
abundant vegetation includes desert fan palms, a jacaranda, and a
variety of citrus trees.

Page 298: Entrance to La Petite Maison, the Gae Aulenti–
designed guest house at the end of the garden. The pergola,
designed by Madison Cox, is supported by palm trunks.

Page 299: Interior of La Petite Maison. Dried leaf above the
mantlepiece by Stuart Thornton. Photographs by OBERTO GILI.

295

PUTTING MY ENERGIES INTO MAKING HOMES *and gardens, imagining how they would turn out, and finding ways to improve them has been a central part of my life. Of all the gardens I have created, I would say that Ain Kassimou is the one that comes closest to my idea of happiness. Sometimes, as I wander here alone or in someone's company, my imagination flies back to the garden of my childhood, in Florence. I used to sneak out of my bed, at night, and wander down to the end of the garden. Just for the thrill of it. In the darkness I could hear all the invisible presences. That's when I first became aware that gardens breathe and are alive, just as we are. One is never really "done" with a garden, just as one is never "done" with life. Day by day and step by step, one just keeps on finding new and clever ways to make them flourish, both in sunshine and in storm.*

Gardeners' hats and mixed roses from the property. Photograph by OBERTO GILI.

DEDICATION

To Ginevra
M. A.

To Costanza, Theodora, Matilde, and Ondina
M. C. C.

ACKNOWLEDGMENTS

The two Marellas would like to extend thank-yous to the many people who made this book possible. To our editor at Rizzoli, Dung Ngo, and to the exceptional team he put together: Mary Shanahan, who designed this book so beautifully, and Philip Reeser who has been superbly in charge of the photo research. Thank you to Roberto Calasso, our Italian publisher and friend, who has backed up this project since the very beginning. We are infinitely grateful to author and historian Benedetta Craveri, a lifelong friend who has egged us both on and given us wise suggestions. Thank you to photographer Oberto Gili who made himself available for a couple of last-minute shoots in Piedmont and for his many beautiful images. And thank you to all the other photographers—Alexandre Bailhache, Eric Boman, Franco Calosso, Marina Cicogna, Wanda Gawronska, Milton Gendel, François Halard, and Priscilla Rattazzi—who, with their talent, have contributed in a substantial way to the making of this book. We are grateful to the archives of Enrico d'Assia, Erwin Blumenfeld, Henry Clarke, Robert Doisneau, Arturo Ghergo, Benno Graziani, Philippe Halsman, Robert Knudsen, Camilla Pecci Blunt McGrath, and Ugo Mulas. This book would not have been complete without contributions from the Condé Nast archive, which includes the work of René Bouché, Henry Clarke, Clifford Coffin, Horst P. Horst, Ray "Scotty" Morrison, Irving Penn, and Karen Radkai. Thank you to Earl McGrath, and to Sebastian White who put us back in touch with him. And thank you also to photographer and longtime friend Marina Schintz, our link to the Blumenfeld archive. An affectionate thank you to Bloum Cardenas of the Niki Charitable Art Foundation for allowing us to publish photographs of Niki de Saint Phalle's Tarot Garden. We are deeply grateful to the foundations of Richard Avedon, Irving Penn, and Andy Warhol, as well as to the Cecil Beaton Studio Archive at Sotheby's and the Truman Capote Literary Trust. We also acknowledge the late George Plimpton for giving Marella Agnelli the opportunity to document her recollections for his book *Truman Capote*—a source that recently helped spur memories of a distant time.

Thank you to editor and friend Caroline Press, who read through and corrected the first draft of the book. And to the fashion historian Sofia Gnoli, a lifelong friend, whom we consulted for this book. A momentous thank you to all those who contributed with their personal experiences and recollections: Maria Sole Agnelli Theodorani, Lucien de Bourcy, Madison Cox, Federico Forquet, Peter Marino, Paolo Pejrone, Roberto Peregalli, Mario d'Urso, and our late and much missed friend Gae Aulenti as well as Alberto Pinto. Nicola Caracciolo, brother and father of the authors, has contributed in a fundamental way to all historical facts relating to the memoir of Marella Agnelli's childhood and youth whilst Ettore Rosboch von Wolkenstein contributed with recollections from the 1960s onward. Thank you to John Elkann for initiating this project and for backing it up where needed. And to Ginevra Elkann Gaetani for cheering us on. Last but not least we would like to thank Paola Montaldo for her invaluable help throughout. And Tiziana Russi, Larissa Oprea, and Angelica Federici, for their assistance along the way.

Flower room at Ain Kassimou, Marrakech. Photograph by
ERIC BOMAN.

Page 2: Portrait in strapless: Marella Agnelli, New York,
December 16, 1953. Photograph by RICHARD AVEDON.

Page 4: Marella Agnelli's bedroom at Villar Perosa, with sage-
green quilted silk on the Louis XV Piedmont bed and a checkered
taffeta baldachin, 1967. Photograph by HORST P. HORST.

THIS BOOK WAS DESIGNED BY MARY SHANAHAN

IMAGE CREDITS

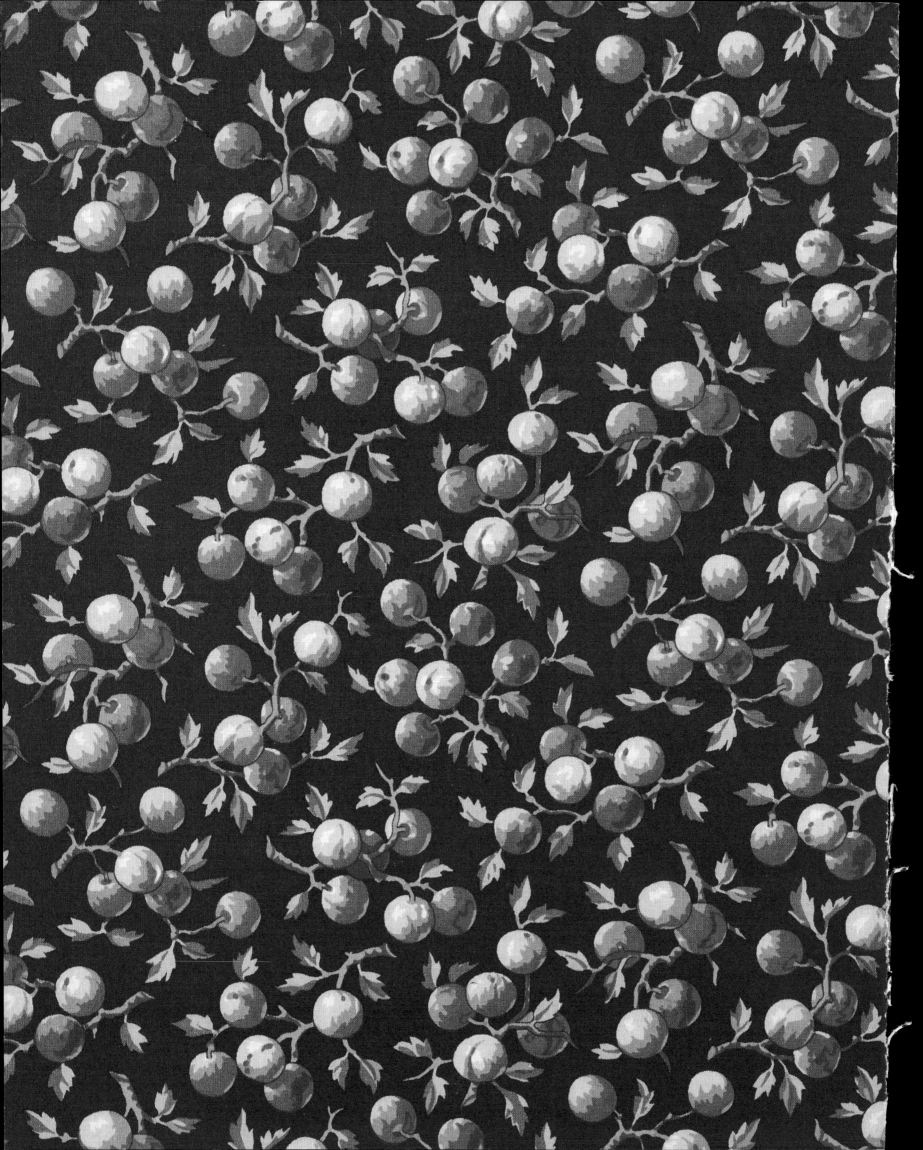